W9-AVZ-997

Barbara Carnes

Making eLearning

S T I C K

Techniques for Easy and Effective
Transfer of Technology-Supported Training

ASTD
PRESS

© 2012 the American Society for Training & Development and Barbara Carnes

All rights reserved. Printed in the United States of America.

16 15 14 13 12   1 2 3 4 5 6 7 8 9 10

No part of this publication may be reproduced, distributed, or transmitted in any form or by any means, including photocopying, recording, or other electronic or mechanical methods, without the prior written permission of the publisher, except in the case of brief quotations embodied in critical reviews and certain other noncommercial uses permitted by copyright law. For permission requests, please go to www.copyright.com, or contact Copyright Clearance Center (CCC), 222 Rosewood Drive, Danvers, MA 01923 (telephone: 978.750.8400, fax: 978.646.8600).

ASTD Press is an internationally renowned source of insightful and practical information on workplace learning and performance topics, including training basics, evaluation and return-on-investment, instructional systems development, e-learning, leadership, and career development.

Ordering information: Books published by ASTD Press can be purchased by visiting ASTD's website at store.astd.org or by calling 800.628.2783 or 703.683.8100.

Library of Congress Control Number: 2012940629
ISBN-10: 1-56286-847-0
ISBN-13: 978-1-56286-847-5

ASTD Press Editorial Staff
Director: Glenn Saltzman
Community of Practice Manager, Learning Technologies: Justin Brusino
Associate Editor: Stephanie Castellano
Design and Production: Marisa Kelly
Cover Design: Ana Foreman

Printed by Versa Press, Inc., East Peoria, IL, www.versapress.com.

Table of Contents

Preface

I have been teaching online, writing university online classes, and designing corporate e-learning for quite a few years now. I have produced many courses that I'm proud of, and a few…well, there were lessons learned. I have received positive feedback often. I know that many other e-learning developers like myself produce e-learning that follows good instructional design principles, and that they seek out techniques to make the learning experience a positive one for the learner. So I was surprised at the many negative comments about e-learning that I began receiving in a university online class I teach. The students, who are mid-career professionals taking the class as part of their degree requirements for an MBA or a master's degree in leadership, report that their experiences with e-learning are about "getting through the class." While a few mentioned that they learned something, the vast majority said that their experience with e-learning is to "check the box" to get credit for the class, but they don't learn much, and what's worse, they don't expect to. A surprising number of them shared tricks such as clicking through slides at a rapid pace, just to finish. One person even said her supervisor told them to click through the slides without reading them! Only one or two of my mid-career students reported that they are actually using what they learned in e-learning courses to help them do their jobs better. Why do so few learners report actually having learned and using what they learned in e-learning? Why do so many just try to get through e-learning? Isn't the focus of all workplace learning, including that which takes place in a virtual environment, to learn skills that can be applied to job performance? These critical questions were my inspiration for writing this book.

When Dora Johnson and I wrote *Making Training Stick* in 1988, it was the first book on training transfer—ever. Our focus in that book was on reinforcement techniques after face-to-face training. No one had heard of e-learning then, and no one thought much about what happens before training either. A few years later Mary Broad and John Newstrom, in their book *Transfer of Training*, identified three critical time periods that are important for training transfer: before, during, and after training. They also identified three critical roles in training: the trainee, the trainer, and the trainee's manager.

Today many more workplace learning professionals understand the importance of the trainee's manager in transforming learning into performance. Many more classroom trainers today also understand and use strategies before and after face-to-face training to encourage application of skills back on the job. But there does not seem to be the same level of understanding or action regarding manager involvement in trainees' e-learning, or strategies and techniques before and after online learning that support application to the job.

Since *Making Training Stick* was written, many academic empirical research studies have explored various factors that contribute to higher levels of training transfer. *Making Learning Stick* (2010) presents a process model for training transfer that is based on these studies, as well as techniques to increase transfer that can be applied no matter what the mode of delivery. However, most of the research on which the book is based was conducted on face-to-face training.

Formal and informal surveys of trainers and of trainees have unearthed many reasons why e-learning participants are often disengaged and fail to apply what they have learned back on the job. Perhaps one key reason is that in face-to-face classes the trainer interacts with trainees and therefore has a more personal interest in and control over the participants' success. Such levels of personalization are not easily reached with e-learning. It is designed and developed, then made available to learners who for the most part remain faceless to the trainer. A survey conducted by Knowledge Advisors found that of more than 5,000 working adults, only nine percent reported that they actually apply what they learn with positive results (Mattox, 2012). In another study, when end-of-course evaluations—50 percent of the courses were e-learning courses—were matched with follow-up evaluations two months later, less than 50 percent of the learning was being used on the job (Bontis, Hardy, and Mattox, 2011). While these findings indicate progress from the widely-quoted Research Institute of America estimate, that after just six days of training only 28 percent of the learning content is retained (Carnes and Johnson, 1988), most would agree that there is considerable room for improvement.

This is not a book about how to design e-learning or live virtual training. There are many good books and classes on this subject. This is a book about how to enhance and add to existing designs to promote application of the skills learned. After all, if participants learn the skills and knowledge taught in training but don't apply them in their jobs, has anything really been accomplished? The techniques in this book require relatively little time and cost to develop, and the payoff for using them can be enormous.

Support from key influencers in an organization is the best way to achieve lasting change of any type, including transferring learning into job performance. Some organizations are ready for this type of change and are developing cultures that foster higher levels of learning transfer; others are not. Regardless of where an organization is in the training transfer culture change curve, the concepts and techniques in this book can be incorporated into new or existing training programs. They can be used as part of an overall learning transfer strategy or they can be used one by one, by individual developers and instructors.

Who Should Read This Book?

Anyone who is interested in the application of workplace learning to job performance will find this book useful.

Chief learning officers, senior human resources leaders, and managers or directors of training

...will be interested in the Transfer of Technology-Supported Training Model in particular, as well as some of the Techniques to Integrate Education (TIEs).

Designers and developers of e-learning, and instructors of virtual classes

…will be interested in adding the TIEs in this book to training they are developing or have already developed.

External consultants, instructors, and designers
…will be able to use the Transfer of Technology-Supported Training Model and the TIEs in this book to provide added value for their clients.

Training coordinators
…will be interested in adding some of the TIEs to their current e-learning courses and linking them with their Learning Management Systems.

Instructors of university or secondary education online classes
…will be able to use some of the TIEs to reinforce their online classes.

Acknowledgments

I received support and encouragement for this book from a lot of people in various areas of my life, and for this I am truly grateful. My friend Kerry Robinson provided a teacher's perspective and the "Do Now" idea. Linda Bardol, one of the most experienced and expert virtual instructors I know, gave helpful feedback on all aspects of the book, especially the live virtual instructions. Betsy Burnett and Beverly Berner provided a bit of balance in my life for which I am extremely grateful. Jim Kirkpatrick also provided very helpful feedback and ideas to expand several areas in my narrative. My client and friend Charles Albach and his team at Washington University Medical School provide ongoing inspiration for e-learning ideas. Clyde Jenkins provided an e-learning developer's point of view, Greg Damron gave some good trainer feedback and created some of the graphics, and Cara Koen did her usual cleanup of my drafts and sketches, especially the Transfer of Technology-Supported Training Model. Thank you!

 **Chapter 1**

Introduction: E-Learning and Training Transfer

Virtual training, also referred to as *online learning,* has existed in some form or another for over 40 years. Most would agree it has revolutionized the way learning is delivered. Organizations spend over $40 billion annually on technology-supported training initiatives. Nearly 20 percent of training courses in the United States are currently offered at a distance, and this rate is increasing. Recent surveys by the American Society for Training & Development and others indicate that while traditional face-to-face instruction will always have a place in workplace learning, the number of participant hours devoted to technology-based formal training is trending upward, taking up more than 30 percent of total training hours. Global Fortune 500 companies, who typically are early adopters of new trends, report that they provide 40 percent of their training via technology-based methods (ASTD, 2011).

Seventy three percent of organizations use online delivery for the majority of their compliance or mandatory training, according to a recent survey from *E-Learning!* magazine (2011). Seventy one percent use virtual classrooms or video broadcasting for company communication and training. Fifty nine percent of desktop application and other IT-related training is done online. The type of training for which online delivery is least used is customer service, but even online training in this area is a healthy 36 percent.

The use of online learning is increasing. In a recent survey of learning executives that appeared in *E-Learning!* magazine, 49 percent of respondents indicated that they plan to increase their investment in learning technologies, and 57 percent will increase their e-learning initiatives (2011).

Development of virtual training usually commands a hefty investment of time and money. It is critical, therefore, to explore ways to increase its effectiveness so that as much of it as possible is transferred to the job and shows up in improved job performance.

What Is Online Learning?

Alternatives to instructor-led learning have existed for many years. In the 1840s a business instructor in Great Britain sent assignments to his students by mail. They completed the work and sent it back to him, and the first modern distance education program was born. Universities offered correspondence courses for at least 150 years before recently replacing them with e-learning courses.

To the average person on the street, *e-learning* can mean anything from conference calls to formal coursework with graphics, video, and testing. Most workplace learning professionals have a narrower definition, but there are still some different interpretations of the term bouncing around the training industry.

Training or Learning?

Distinguishing between *training* and *learning* (never mind e-learning and live virtual training) can be a long discussion. Some people prefer not to use the term *training*, believing it refers to animal training. Others prefer to use the word *learning* when referring to what the recipient does, which is assimilating information and acquiring skills. That there is a difference between training and learning is readily acknowledged. However, in the discussions of training transfer strategies in this book, these two terms will be used interchangeably. The term *e-learning* has become popular probably because it is more appealing to the ear than *e-training*.

Time and Place

To clarify what is meant by e-learning it is helpful to think in terms of time and place. With traditional face-to-face training, instructor and trainees are in the same place, at the same time. Learning content and activities are usually confined to this specified time and place, although there may be some supportive strategies before and after the learning event. This of course is not e-learning.

Training that takes place at the same time and where trainer and trainees are in different places is known by many terms. Some call it e-learning, others call it virtual classes, still others call it *live virtual training* or *virtual instructor-led training*. Often this type of training is also referred to as a *webinar*, much as a face-to-face class may be referred to as a seminar. By whatever name, this type of training is conducted using an electronic classroom platform that allows learners and instructors in different places to participate at the same time. Interaction is accomplished via features such as chat, breakout rooms, polling, and activity icons. The term *live virtual training* seems the best term to capture this increasingly popular form of training. A *webinar*, on the other hand, should be considered the virtual equivalent of a seminar, shorter in duration and with much less interaction than a live virtual training class.

The term **live virtual training** *is used in this book to refer to training that is delivered synchronously to multiple participants in different locations. Training that is delivered at different times and in different places is referred to here as* e-learning. *The techniques in this book focus on both self-paced e-learning and live virtual training.*

Training that takes place at different times and in different places began as *computer-based training* or CBT. It was delivered to learners via various electronic platforms. Today the means of delivery has changed, but the concept of having course materials available on demand is still the same. Now web-based, this type of on-demand learning is self-guided; that is without a trainer, facilitator, or coordinator to monitor, guide, or instruct. It is this type of learning that is referred to here as *e-learning*. The techniques in this book focus on both self-paced e-learning and live virtual training.

Figure 1-1. Technology-Supported Training: Time and Place

Same Time/Different Place	Different Time/Different Place

Live virtual training: Instructor is present. Content may include interactive learning activities.	E-learning: Access to learning content is on demand. Content may include video segments, learner interactivity with the learning content, and testing. Instructorless on-demand learning.
Same Time/Same Place	**Different Time/Same Place**

Traditional classroom learning with an instructor, perhaps augmented by out-of-class activities.	Learning lab: Individual learners participate in learning activities in central location, perhaps with administrator or coach available.

Inspired by: Thompson, L. (2008). *The Mind and Heart of the Negotiator,* 4th ed.

Transfer of Training

Training transfer is defined as the application of on-the-job knowledge, skills, and attitudes learned from training as well as the subsequent use of them over time. The e-learning module or live virtual class may be engaging, and the learners, subject matter experts, and other stakeholders may be satisfied with it. The course is loaded onto the Learning Management System (LMS), trainees take it and receive credit for it, but they also need to try out and begin using the knowledge and skills they have learned in training back on the job.

E-Learning Technologies

Within this time and place framework, different technologies are used to deliver e-learning and live virtual training: authoring applications, Internet and intranet systems, Learning Management Systems, virtual training classroom platforms, social media platforms, mobile learning, QR codes, and so on. Each of these technologies and tools has unique characteristics that make it useful for the delivery and support of training. Each of them also can be employed to support the transfer of training back to the job. The Techniques to Integrate Education (TIEs) in this book make use of many of these technologies as a "means to the end goal," which is increased application of skills learned in training. However, keep in mind that specific technologies may work well in some organizational settings and IT environments and not in others. The tools, techniques, and strategies in this book can be employed using a variety of different technologies depending on the organization's resources and preferences.

Learning Management Systems

The LMS technology deserves special attention here because it can be used to facilitate many of the techniques and strategies suggested in this book. A recent survey on LMS features conducted by BizLibrary indicates that most organizations use their LMS primarily for administration (Osborn, 2010). Three additional sets of LMS features have emerged and are being used increasingly: test and survey tools, collaboration tools, and mobile learning. All of these LMS features, including administrative functions, can and should be employed to support better levels of training transfer. LMSs also allow participation to be tracked and therefore provide accountability, which is important for reinforcement and on-the-job application.

Learning Is a Process, Not an Event

The focus of workplace learning is almost always on the learning event, whether delivered face-to-face, in a live virtual class, via e-learning, or through a blended format. Yet research in learning theory and training transfer points out that what happens before and after the learning event also strongly influences whether the learning is retained and used. Therefore the process of designing and, in the case of live virtual classes, instructing, should include activities and techniques to be used before and after the participant takes the training.

Blessings and Challenges of Online Learning

There are many advantages of self-paced e-learning and live virtual training. Learners can access the training program at their convenience, in the comfort of their own workspace, and using their own devices. E-learning and live virtual training eliminate the need for travel to faraway places or even to the next building. If the learner misses a live virtual session, he or she can usually access a recording of it. The advantages of these learning modes to the organization include elimination of travel time and expense, as well as the consistency of learning content from session to session, instructor to instructor.

Self-paced e-learning, and to some extent live virtual training, allows the learner to have more control over her learning than she would have in traditional face-to-face training. E-learning courses in most cases allow the learner to control the pace of the learning and in some cases, the sequence of the learning modules too. Higher levels of learner control are generally considered to be an advantage of e-learning. However, at least one study has found that when the learning content is complex and learners are allowed to control the pace and sequence, the levels of learning transfer are significantly lower.

There are also distinct disadvantages associated with e-learning and live virtual training. The trainees' workspace can be invaded at any time with incoming emails, telephone calls, co-workers who stop by, and a calendar full of meetings and other commitments. That comfy workspace most likely also has various distractions sitting on their desks (or desktops). Also, the e-learning module is impersonal, without opportunities to ask questions and have them answered. Live virtual training does provide opportunities to ask questions, but lacks nonverbal cues such as facial expressions and body language (though it does accommodate tone and inflection) so the trainer cannot respond to trainees who are reluctant to raise their virtual hand. Trainees' keyboarding skills may also limit their ability to type questions via chat.

While the benefits may outweigh the disadvantages, it is important to keep these disadvantages in mind. Many of the techniques in this book were designed specifically to help the trainer, participant, and manager overcome some of the disadvantages inherent in both online mediums.

Cool Stuff or Good Enough?

Just a few years ago most e-learning consisted of slides that had been adapted from live instruction. Today's rapid design tools make it easier than ever to create graphics, animations, simulations, video, games, and other techniques intended to increase learner engagement. While these techniques can be quite effective, they sometimes distract from good, solid instructional content. Be wary of incorporating too many bells and whistles in e-learning, and when considering a new tool or technique, consider whether it really supports the learning objectives.

A "good enough" training course provides the framework for achieving the learning objectives and transferring training to the job. A good enough design includes some flashy tools—enough sparkle to keep learners engaged—but they all serve a firm purpose. A good enough training design—and trainer— doesn't have to use the latest and greatest technology. They just need to produce the desired results: on-the-job application and performance. This "good enough" training design is not about being lazy or less interested in the final product. It's about keeping the end goal in mind and using resources wisely.

Be wary of incorporating too many bells and whistles in e-learning, and when considering a new tool or technique, consider whether it really supports the learning objectives.

The Evolving Roles of the Trainer

An inevitable result of the increasing use of technology-mediated training is that there are new roles for the trainer. Some of these include:

❖ developer of e-learning content

❖ facilitator of virtual classes

❖ provider of follow-up support

❖ bridge-builder between subject matter expert and learners

❖ encourager of peer-to-peer and manager-employee learning.

How Do You Know if It's Sticking?

James and Wendy Kirkpatrick's recent writing on evaluation of training discusses *return-on-expectations* (ROE). The first step in the process of determining whether training has transferred is to identify the expectations of the sponsors of the training. What outcomes are stakeholders expecting to see as a result of the training? Identify expectations through interviews, questionnaires, meetings, and focus groups. Next, measure and compare the actual training outcomes against these expectations. It is only through this process of identifying expectations and assessing training outcomes that there can be any satisfaction that the training is accomplishing its intended goal.

There are many ways to measure training outcomes. To discuss them all at length goes beyond the scope of this book, but here are some basic approaches:

❖ Survey the supervisors of the trainees: What changes have they observed in the targeted skills and behaviors since the training? What skills are participants using? Survey participants and ask the same questions.

❖ Investigate by observing some trainees performing their work, on the shop floor or in a call center, for example. A trainer's observation will probably be more detailed, accurate, and useful than another person's observation. Or enlist a "mystery shopper"—an internal individual who may or may not be a member of the learning and development staff but is likely to be unknown to trainees. This person is in a position to observe firsthand whether the participants are using the skills from their training.

❖ Investigate training outcomes at multiple post-training time periods: three weeks after training, six weeks after training, and three months after training. Some trainees may not have had an opportunity to use the training shortly after it occurred. Others may have used it right away but forgotten about it later.

ROI Made Easy

The next step after evaluating training transfer is to determine whether the benefits of the training are worth the investment of resources. A return-on-investment (ROI) calculation should always be preceded by an evaluation of training transfer. There are many formulas and methods for calculating ROI and numerous good books on the subject. Here is the basic method for arriving at a figure that more or less represents the return on training investment:

❖ Add up the costs of the training. Include indirect costs, such as a portion of the developer's salary, and the proportionate cost of authoring systems or live classroom platforms, as well as any direct costs such as per-learner LMS costs.

❖ Assess or estimate the results of the training. How much more revenue did the organization gain as a result of these improved skills? How much did the organization save as a result? This can involve some guesswork and tricky calculations to arrive at a dollars-and-cents estimate of how trainees' improved skills affected key organization metrics.

❖ Once the cost figure and results figure have been determined, divide the costs by the results to arrive at the return-on-investment.

For some good tools and resources on training ROI do a browser search on "training ROI calculator" or "return on training investment."

Figure 1-2. Training Transfer Process Model

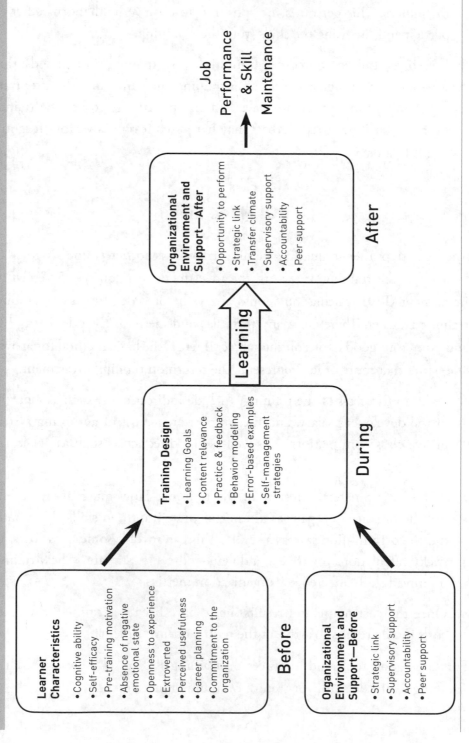

Learner Characteristics
- Cognitive ability
- Self-efficacy
- Pre-training motivation
- Absence of negative emotional state
- Openness to experience
- Extroverted
- Perceived usefulness
- Career planning
- Commitment to the organization

Training Design
- Learning Goals
- Content relevance
- Practice & feedback
- Behavior modeling
- Error-based examples
- Self-management strategies

Organizational Environment and Support—After
- Opportunity to perform
- Strategic link
- Transfer climate
- Supervisory support
- Accountability
- Peer support

Organizational Environment and Support—Before
- Strategic link
- Supervisory support
- Accountability
- Peer support

Job Performance & Skill Maintenance

Learning

Before

During

After

© Carnes and Associates, Inc.

How to Use This Book

This book and its collection of techniques can be used a few different ways, depending on the reader's reading and learning styles, time constraints, and specific needs. Although some may enjoy reading it cover to cover, others will want to use it as a reference, taking it off the shelf and reviewing it when making e-learning stick becomes top of mind. Many trainers who have used previous "stick" books suggest reading Section 1 from beginning to end and reviewing Techniques to Integrate Education (TIEs) as needed, especially before designing, launching, conducting, or refreshing a live virtual training event or e-learning. Choose the TIEs for before, during, and after the learning event that are the best fit for the learning content, delivery platform, trainer, and organizational culture. TIEs may also be modified and adapted to fit specific needs and available technologies. For more techniques and downloadable resources to use in e-learning programs, please go to *www.makeelearningstick.com*.

The Training Transfer Process

Many empirical research studies have been conducted regarding factors that support transfer of training. The Training Transfer Process Model shown on the previous page, first introduced in *Making Learning Stick*, is based on many of these studies. The end result and goal of training (see the right side of the model) is improved job performance and skill maintenance; that is, the transfer of the training to the job. The categories of factors that support this end result are Learner Characteristics, Organizational Environment and Support Before Training, the Training Design, and Organizational Environment and Support After Training. Within each of these categories, specific factors are listed that help achieve successful training transfer. Each factor is supported by multiple research studies.

Learner Characteristics

Cognitive ability, in the workplace learning industry, refers to intellectual ability. People with higher cognitive ability are better able to retain information and thus transfer it to the workplace.

Self-efficacy is the belief an individual has about his ability to perform a particular task. Closely related to self-confidence, individuals with higher levels of self-efficacy are more likely to transfer skills learned in training to their jobs.

Pre-training motivation refers to the learner's interest in learning the content and applying it to his job. It should be noted that internal motivation to learn and apply the learning is more likely to produce transfer than external motivation. External motivators, such as rewards, were not found to produce higher levels of transfer to the job. One exception to this rule, however, is the motivator of performance appraisals: If applying the learning content was directly linked to the learner's performance appraisal, he was more likely to transfer the learning to the job.

Some learner personality characteristics were found to be related to better training transfer. Learners *without negative attitudes* were more likely to transfer training. Trainees who were *open to new experiences* have also been found to be better able to capitalize on learning successes and to acquire skills faster.

Extroversion—specifically the tendency to verbalize thoughts and feelings—has been thought to be related to training transfer. This is not to say that only extroverts are more likely to transfer learning to the job, however. It simply suggests that trainees who tend to be more introverted benefit from having extroverts in training with them, because extroverts tend to verbalize strategies and applications, leading to more "cognitive sharing" so that all training participants benefit. More research is needed to support this theory, but it does seem reasonable.

Learners are more likely to transfer learning to the job when they *perceive the usefulness of the training*. When trainees perceive that the training will help them improve their job performance, and that their new skills will be relatively easy to use on the job, they are more likely to transfer their training to the job.

Trainees who create and update *career plans* for themselves are more likely to transfer learning to their jobs because they perceive potential benefits more accurately than those who are less active in their career planning.

Learners who identify with workplace groups (departments and work units) and are *committed to their organization* tend to be interested learners who want to gain and use their new skills and knowledge at work.

Training Design

Learning goals or objectives that are explicitly communicated to trainees tell them what level of performance is expected as a result of the training. When trainees receive the objectives in advance of the training, they are likely to have higher levels of transfer.

Training goals, materials, and practices that are specific to the trainee's job duties are more likely to be applied to the job. Such *content relevance* has been found in many studies to be highly correlated to transfer.

When participants have opportunities to *practice skills in the training and receive feedback* on their performance, they are more likely to transfer the training to their jobs. Specifically, mental rehearsal ("what would you do if" scenarios) and behavioral practice strategies (role playing) have the strongest correlations with transfer. Distributing practice sessions throughout the training rather than concentrating them in one part of the learning event also leads to higher levels of transfer.

Behavior modeling—that is, demonstrating to participants the desired performance or behavior—enhances transfer. *Error-based examples* are the flip side of behavior modeling. Participants are shown examples of ineffective behaviors, or "mixed examples"—demonstrations of both desirable and undesirable performance. Trainees who participate in these types of demonstrations are more likely to transfer their learning to the job.

Instructional strategies aimed at helping participants *self-manage* their behavior when they return to work have been found to increase training transfer. Two specific strategies are goal-setting and the self-management technique called *relapse prevention*. Both strategies prompt participants to envision how they will use their new skills and develop an operational strategy for doing so.

Organizational Environment and Support—
Before and After Training

An organization's environment can do much to further training transfer for its employees. It is important to ensure that trainees can perceive alignment of the training content (the *strategic link*) with the organization's strategic direction. Resources provided to trainees before and after training, such as job aids, strategically placed posters, newsletter reminders, and so on, are highly useful in training transfer as they prompt trainees to use their new skills. Another component of a positive *transfer climate* is *peer and supervisor support* in the form of feedback, encouragement, and incentives to apply the newly-learned skills. Supervisors can significantly influence trainees' transfer of skills to the job. Specific activities, such as discussing the new learning with the trainee, participating in part of the training, and providing encouragement and coaching to trainees, result in better training transfer. Trainees' supervisors should also be encouraged to modify their employees' normal workload to allow them to take the training uninterrupted and to practice new skills on the job. Trainees' peers can also exert a strong influence on the transfer of skills and knowledge. Communicating with peers prior to a learning event helps them understand the value of the learning and specific ways it could be utilized on the job. Sharing ideas afterward about course content, applications, challenges, and successes reinforces the skills and knowledge gained from the training in a context that is specific to the trainees' jobs.

Positive transfer climates also have a system in place which rewards correct usage of new skills and behaviors, and initiates remedial assistance when the skills are not used. Such *accountability* can be accomplished through performance expectations and reviews, requiring learners to report afterward on their training experience, and conversely, providing sanctions for failure to use learned skills on the job. Several studies have found that the most important reason training transfers is the *opportunity to use* the new skills as soon as possible after completing the training.

Transfer of Technology-Supported Training

The research that supports the Training Transfer Process Model was conducted almost entirely on face-to-face training. An exhaustive search for similar empirical studies on transfer from technology-supported training revealed far fewer results. While some interesting studies were found, the volume of research published on this topic was disappointing. No doubt as time goes on this body of research will expand, just as the volume of research on the transfer of face-to-face training has expanded as interest in the topic has grown.

Many of the principles behind the transfer of face-to-face training hold true for the transfer of e-learning, although how they are executed may vary significantly depending on the training delivery platform. The Transfer of Technology-Supported Training Model found below represents a combination of factors supported by research on face-to-face training that can applied to e-learning, and factors supported by research on the transfer of e-learning.

Figure 1-3. Transfer of Technology-Supported Training Model

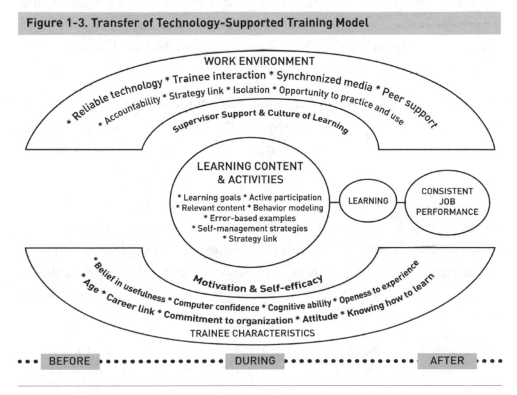

© Carnes and Associates, Inc.

Learning Content and Activities

Learning goals. Stating the goals, objectives, and purpose of the training, in learner-friendly language, helps the learner understand what they are supposed to learn and why. While instructional objectives are an important aspect of designing training, the objectives should be restated to learners in user-friendly language at the beginning of the training.

Active participation. It is well-known that lecturing alone does not result in the best learning in a face-to-face environment. Lecturing in virtual training environments, or requiring learners to read extensive texts, also makes for unpromising results. Instead, learners should be actively involved throughout the course through the use of techniques like frequent questions, discussions, polls, quizzes, content links, games, and simulations.

Relevant content. Many subject matter experts strive to include as much information as possible about their topic and how to perform their skill. However, too much information leads to information overload, and the result of this is that the trainee isn't able to learn, retain, or use any of it. Learning content must be relevant for the learning outcome, whether for skill acquisition, knowledge, or both.

Behavior modeling. No matter what the mode of delivery, behavior modeling is important for learner retention and transfer. A video clip, photo, or sketch can provide effective models in the virtual world just as they do in face-to-face training.

Error-based examples. This technique involves showing trainees how *not* to perform the skill. It is one of the least-known instructional strategies that have been found to support better transfer. The error-based example must be different enough from the correct example so that it is easy for the trainee to distinguish. When learners see, read, or hear about the ineffective use of the targeted skill in addition to its effective use, they are more likely to use what they learn.

Self-management strategies. Fewer than five percent of e-learning courses contain action plans, yet research has found that when supported and reinforced by supervisors and peers, these self-management tools can be very effective. Notes and fill-in tools that are part of many authoring systems can be helpful here.

Strategy link. When trainees are able to understand during the training how the skills they are learning will support the organization's mission and strategic objectives, they are more likely to apply their learning to their job. A few comments or a short video can provide the necessary communication to make this link.

Work Environment

Two overarching elements in the work environment play a large role in determining whether or not trainees apply their learning to their jobs: supervisor support and a culture of learning within the organization or work unit. These characteristics are also related to many of the other factors in the work environment that affect training transfer.

Supervisor support. The trainee's supervisor can be encouraged to support the training and assist the participant with application through the use of tools such as video clips, webpages, and social media.

Culture of learning. "The speed of the leaders is the speed of the gang." When senior leaders show their support for learning through examples such as requirements for development within performance evaluations, signals about manager priorities, support for experimentation without fear of the consequences of failure, and incentives for skill application, trainees are more likely to transfer their learning to their jobs.

Reliable technology. Trainees become frustrated when links don't work, the program stalls, they aren't able to access the program, they find themselves "kicked out of" the electronic classroom, or other features of the training don't work. With each failure of technology, the participant is less likely to stay engaged with the program.

Trainee interaction. Virtual activities that provide opportunities for trainees to interact with one another result in higher levels of learning transfer. This interaction can take many forms: threaded discussions, learning communities devoted to a specific topic or class, real time interaction via instant messaging, or conference calls. The interactions should be structured, and the technology should support the structure and vice versa.

Synchronized media. To facilitate and support trainee interaction, it is important to have technologies that interface with each other. While it is possible to set up interaction technologies (also known as social media) that are not technically integrated with an e-learning course or live virtual training platform, the more steps that are needed for access, the less likely it will be used. Ideally, the training class will contain links to threaded discussions and online learning communities and the Learning Management System will be able to track participation in them. Learning Management Systems increasingly provide social media features, the option to call up live Internet sessions, simulations and games, and YouTube videos.

Peer support. Participants who interact with their fellow employees gain valuable information and motivation that influences their transfer of the learning. Social media and other electronic technologies can create convenient opportunities for these peer-to-peer interactions.

Accountability. Being responsible to someone or even something is a powerful motivator of behavior. Trainees who are held accountable by their managers and peers for practicing and using their newly learned skills are much more likely to practice and use them.

Strategy link. When trainees are able to understand how what they are about to learn and have learned will support the organization's mission and strategic objectives, they are more likely to apply their learning to their job. A few comments or a short video can provide the necessary communication to make this link.

Isolation. The participant may have the best intentions for focusing on the virtual training or e-learning class, but then they see an email come through that competes for their attention, or a well-meaning co-worker stops by with a question. Once distracted, most learners find it hard to reconnect with the class. One study found that, once interrupted, a learner will take 30 percent more time to complete the training—if they complete the training at all.

Include instructions in registration emails and initial e-learning screens to close all other applications (including instant messaging) and to turn off phones.

Opportunity to practice and use. "If you don't use it, you lose it." Participants must practice and use their learning as soon as possible. The more time that passes between learning the new skill and using it, the more likely that it will not be used. Scheduling time and opportunities to practice or use the new skill should be encouraged within the training. Trainees' managers should be reminded to help them schedule time to do this.

Trainee Characteristics

Two overarching characteristics of participants strongly influence training transfer: motivation and self-efficacy. These also play a role in other trainee characteristics that are part of this model.

Motivation. Internal and external trainee motivation, before, during, and after training plays a key role in transfer of training to the job. Internal motivation to learn and use the training may help propel the trainee toward learning and use but will likely falter without support from the environment. Motivation to learn and use the learning also affects and is affected by openness to experience and links to career progress.

Self-efficacy. Closely related to self-confidence, self-efficacy is an individual's belief that they will be able to learn and perform a task. Many studies point to self-efficacy as an overriding force in training transfer. "You can do it" messages in the registration email and early course slides, as well as success stories from previous participants, can boost learners' self-confidence.

Belief in usefulness. Workplace learners need to see how they will be able to use what they learn. E-learning and live virtual developers should avoid pressure from subject matter experts to include nice-to-know content and verify with target population representatives which content is need-to-know.

Computer confidence. If participants are uncertain about using the technology associated with the training, the learning is less likely to be applied. While most (but not all) employees in today's workplaces are comfortable using a personal computer, some may not be completely comfortable using technologies associated with live virtual training, such as VoIP (Voice over Internet Protocol), threaded discussion, type-in chat, and virtual breakout groups.

Cognitive ability. Trainees' cognitive abilities affect their levels of learning and how much they apply their learning to the job. This factor is closely related to *knowing how to learn.*

Openness to experience. Trainees who are open to new experiences are better able to capitalize on learning successes, to acquire skills faster, and to transfer the new skills to their jobs. Training courses can set the stage and encourage learners to open their minds as they experience the training.

Age. Younger learners tend to achieve higher levels of learning transfer in technology-supported training because they have been users of related technologies for most, if not all, of their lives.

Career link. Learners who have career plans that they regularly consult and update, and learners who see a link between specific training and their career plans, are more likely to apply their learning to their job performance.

Commitment to the organization. There is a relationship between identification with workplace groups and the desire to gain and use new work-related knowledge. Trainees who have a strong commitment to their organization, or to their team or work unit, are more likely to use in their jobs what they have learned in their training. A popular term closely associated with this is *employee engagement.*

Attitude. Learners with positive mental emotional states—or at least the absence of negative mental emotional states—are more likely to transfer their training. Whether in regard to the training itself, or a general life attitude, positive attitudes support better transfer.

Knowing how to learn. Trainees who have metacognitive skills such as how to focus, self-regulate, and take tests effectively, are better able to learn and transfer technology-assisted training. These types of skills are helpful for participants in face-to-face learning environments too, but due to the increased isolation— physical and psychological—of e-learning and live virtual training, metacognitive skills play a larger role in participants' ability to transfer their learning.

Chapter 2

The Bears, the Bees,
and the Honey

This story has been familiar to trainers for more than two decades:

Once upon a time in the land of human resource development (HRD) there was an organization that relied on the work of bears to produce goods and services, which generated money to pay the taxes that kept the land healthy and well. The organization thrived, the bears were paid well for their work, and the land prospered. The bears worked exceptionally well together. Each knew his job, how each job related to the others, and why each job was important to the overall vision of the organization.

Also in this organization were trainer bees. The bees were very effective in their jobs of assessing needs and developing virtual, face-to-face, and blended learning courses. Each bee, whether she was an instructional designer, instructor, producer, coordinator, or manager, also worked well with others, and knew her job responsibilities.

Everything was going along fine until a change took place that required the bears to learn a new production process very quickly. The trainer bees assessed the need and designed an exceptional blended learning initiative that incorporated an e-learning module and live virtual training. They rolled out the training in record time and trained 50 bears in the new process. The end-of-program evaluations were outstanding. Three weeks later the bees checked back with the bears to see how they were using what they had learned.

They were completely dismayed. While some bears were using the new process and techniques well, many others had returned to their old ways of doing things. The bees knew it was critical that all bears adopt this new process, so the manager bee called a staff meeting. The manager explained the situation and outlined the task: They needed to find a way to help the bears remember what they had learned and apply it back on the job.

The bees buzzed and talked about threatening the bears with demotions and loss of their jobs, but then discarded that idea because they knew it would only cause resistance. They thought about leaving the task to the bears' managers, but they also rejected that idea immediately because they knew that as trainer bees, they would be held accountable for how the bears were using the new skills. They also thought about requiring the bears to complete extra assignments, but said no to this idea too. It was too much like school and the bees knew the bears would resist. Finally the bees discussed leaving the bears alone and being satisfied with the low success rate, but they knew they could solve this problem and they were not willing to give up so soon.

The bees continued to think. They agreed that their training needed to:

❖ fully engage the bears

❖ be immediately relevant to the bears' jobs

❖ clearly connect the training outcomes to the organization's new direction.

The trainer bees asked themselves, "What can we do to make our training interesting and useful to the bears, and make them want to stick with what they learn once they get back to their jobs?"

"Ah-ha!" they answered themselves. "Honey! Honey is something we can make ourselves, it's desired by bears, and it certainly is sticky. We will coat each of our training classes with special honey—techniques to integrate education—so the bears will want to take what they learn back to their jobs."

They tried it. The bears liked it, and more importantly, they started using what they had learned back on their jobs.

And they all worked happily ever after.

The most effective training transfer strategies will incorporate multiple TIEs.

Techniques to Integrate Education (TIEs)

In the story of the bears and the bees, TIEs are the honey that the trainer bees made, which the bears liked, which made the training stick. This book contains TIEs that learning and development and human resource professionals—e-learning designers, live virtual training instructors and producers, learning and development managers, and training coordinators—can use before, during, and after learning classes to make the learning stick. Although some TIEs may lend themselves to particular types of training content (soft skills, technical skills, and so on), most TIEs can be used with any type of content. Likewise, most TIEs can be adapted for a variety of delivery platforms. This book provides step-by-step instructions for use with both e-learning and live virtual training. Most of the TIEs in this book can also be adapted for face-to-face instruction. If there is a situation in which a particular TIE may not be effective, it is noted. You may use the TIEs in this book as is, adapt them, or use them as a springboard to create new TIEs. It should be noted that TIEs are not one-stop solutions, however. The most effective training transfer strategies will incorporate multiple TIEs and other techniques.

To summarize, TIEs are

❖ easy to use

❖ low cost or no cost

❖ usable with new or existing training

❖ appropriate for most training content

❖ adaptable for a variety of technologies

❖ based on training transfer research.

On the opposite page is a summary of the TIEs in this book, indicating whether each is best used *during* an e-learning course or live virtual training, or *before or afterward*. Each TIE is explained in depth in chapter 3. For additional TIEs, refer to my previous books: *Making Learning Stick*, *Making Training Stick*, and *Making Training Stick: A Training Transfer Field Guide*. For more downloadable examples, forms, and other resources, go to *www.makeelearningstick.com*. The Techniques to Integrate Education (TIEs) Table (Figure 2-1) serves as an at-a-glance worksheet for readers considering which TIEs to use before, during, and after training. Figure 2-2 serves as a planning tool for readers considering how to build TIEs into their training programs.

Figure 2-1. Techniques to Integrate Education (TIEs) Table

TIE	Use During Training	Use Before/ After Training	Page Number
Action Learning	x	x	27
Action Plans	x	x	32
Application Checks	x		35
Do Not Disturb	x		38
Do Now	x		42
Feel-Felt-Found	x		44
KISS	x		47
A Little Help From Friends	x	x	50
Live Pilot	x		53
Manager Module		x	56
Note to Self	x	x	58
Picture This	x		60
Pop-Up Reflections	x		62
QR Codes	x	x	65
Sticky Blog		x	68
Sticky Heat Map		x	73
Sticky Kit		x	77
Sticky Learning Community	x	x	81
Sticky Microblog		x	85
Sticky Objectives	x		88
Sticky Wiki		x	92
Strategy Link	x	x	97
Thank-You Note		x	100
Threaded Discussion	x	x	102
Transfer Certificate		x	106
Virtual Tutor	x	x	109
What's Wrong With This Picture?	x		112
Wrap It Up	x		115

Figure 2-2. Checklist for Better Training Transfer

Make sure the training has:	TIE or other technique to be used:
learning goals and objectives easily understood by trainees	
relevant content only	
modeling of skills and behaviors	
self-management strategies such as action plans	
connection with the strategic goals of the organization	
error-based examples, if appropriate (see What's Wrong With This Picture? TIE)	
Pre-class notes or slides that:	**TIE or other technique to be used:**
encourage participants and build their self-confidence that they will be able to learn and apply the skills and knowledge	
connect the class topic with the strategic goals of the organization	
remind participants to close out applications and turn off phones	
explain how this class will help participants do their jobs better	
Pre-class note to trainees' supervisors that:	
asks them to discuss the learning objectives with the trainees	
asks them to arrange opportunities to practice and use the new skills as soon as possible	
asks them to hold the trainees accountable for using the skills on the job	
Follow-up notes or slides that:	**TIE or other technique to be used:**
remind trainees to practice and use what they have learned	
encourage participants and build their self-confidence that they can apply the skills and knowledge they have learned	
suggest they enlist help and support from peers and supervisors	
Follow-up note to trainees' supervisors that:	
asks them to arrange opportunities to practice and use the new skills as soon as possible	
asks them to hold the trainees accountable for using the skills on the job	
encourages them to connect the trainees with others who have taken the class and learned the skill	

Chapter 3

Techniques to Integrate Education (TIEs)

TIE: Action Learning

Action learning is a process by which participants "learn by doing": that is, they acquire and apply knowledge through actions rather than traditional instruction. Research on action learning has shown that action learning programs are at least 30 percent more effective than traditional lecturing. Action learning usually involves opportunities for small groups of individuals to solve real organizational problems while at the same time focusing on their learning. Developed first by Reg Revans in England in the mid-20th century, action learning has evolved into many different forms. But they usually share these characteristics:

❖ Action learning scenarios present a problem, challenge, opportunity, issue, or task. It should be significant and important to the organization, group, or area of expertise.

❖ While the problem can be tackled by an individual, ideally a team of four to six individuals works together to examine and solve an organizational problem. The problem should be relatively complex so that it cannot be solved easily or quickly. The group can be made up of individuals from different areas of the organization, or from the same department.

❖ The action learning process begins by posing questions to clarify the problem and then reflecting on possible solutions. The focus is on the questions and the reflection, which results in learning.

❖ The process generates energy and creativity best when action can be taken and results can be reflected upon. There is equal emphasis on solving the problem and unearthing the learning that occurred during the process of solving it.

Action learning can be used as an activity or key learning strategy within an e-learning course or live virtual training. For example, you may design your training so that the action learning project is used as application practice following the presentation of structured learning content. While originally intended for live teams, action learning projects can be adapted for an online environment, with a focus on either an individual or a team activity.

In a face-to-face environment, most action learning experts recommend a coach to guide participants through the steps of problem analysis, and lead the discussion of how the solution was arrived at. In a virtual environment, a virtual coach could be assigned to the team, or the coaching role might be rotated among team members. As an alternative, a series of coaching questions can be posed so that in effect, the training course becomes the coach.

To use with e-learning

1. Using focus groups, interviews, or surveys of management, identify significant problems in the workplace that would benefit from in-depth analysis and resolution.

2. Determine whether the project should drive the course or the course should drive the project. In other words, should the project be introduced first and the learning content—whether extensive or brief—be provided after the project introduction, as the means to the end? Or should the learning content be presented first with the action learning project appearing at a later point, perhaps as a capstone to the course?

3. Develop a description of the problem to be solved. While a simple text explanation may be sufficient, video recordings from key stakeholders or knowledgeable individuals will add depth and meaning. Hint: Take a video camera to the information-gathering focus group or interviews mentioned in step one.

4. Decide how to assign teams. Action learning is fueled by the synergy of individuals working together. An LMS or training coordinator could assign team members based on when they register for the course, or managers could assign teams based on a specific project or need that must be addressed. While it is not an ideal action learning scenario, individual learners rather than teams could work independently on projects.

5. Incorporate coaching into the action learning project. If a virtual coach will be assigned, identify key points during the project at which the coach should be consulted. Coaching questions can also be incorporated at key points in the action learning process. The questions are meant to encourage participants to critically assess the problem and their attempts to solve it. For example:

   ❖ What assumptions are behind the definition of the problem?

   ❖ What types of feedback have been given to each collaborator?

   ❖ What seems most difficult, so far, in the process?

   ❖ What seems easy? Too easy?

   ❖ What has the planning process been so far? How is it working? Does it need adjusting?

   ❖ What aspects of the learning content come to mind when reflecting on the project work?

   ❖ What aspects of the learning content have been confirmed or observed here?

   ❖ Are there any alternative solutions to this problem? In other words, what's the second right answer?

6. Decide what will be done with the results of the project. Action learning projects work best when the team is empowered to implement the

solution, evaluate results, and make any necessary adjustments. However, this may not be possible, especially in an e-learning environment. Given the situation, what could be done with the results of the action learning?

7. When the project is completed, the course can be revised using another problem or opportunity. The same principles of problem-solving and course content are used.

Action learning projects work best when the team is empowered to implement the solution, evaluate results, and make any necessary adjustments.

Adaptations for live virtual training

1. Determine the best way to incorporate the action learning project for live virtual learning. Several different action learning projects and teams could be supported by a series of live virtual learning events, or the action learning project could be assigned after content has been delivered, as a capstone of the class.

2. When describing the problem to be solved, consider your training platform. For example, if it cannot support video, try using photographs accompanied by audio clips (record a telephone conversation or VOIP technology-assisted meeting).

3. Live virtual training events offer great opportunities for coaching during action learning projects. Coaching questions and feedback could be the focus of live virtual sessions, or you may divide the time between content delivery and project coaching. You may also want to assign a virtual coach to step into this role during the training—someone who is knowledgeable about the project.

Downsides

This TIE may not be effective if:

❖ There is little interest or support from management for forming teams to solve organizational problems, or implementing their solutions.

❖ Project teams do not have the guidance, leadership, or self-direction to move through the problem-solving process.

❖ The training topic does not lend itself to action learning. Topics that may not be a fit include ethics training, harassment prevention, and "how-to" technical training.

❖ The training is being rolled out to large numbers of people, without the resources or opportunities to identify and solve problems.

Variations

❖ Use live virtual sessions for project team meetings, in addition to or instead of learning content delivery. This will be easier if the technology platform allows for breakout groups. Otherwise, learning content can be presented first followed by separate "classes" for each project team, with the trainer rotating among the classrooms.

❖ Develop an avatar to serve as a virtual coach as part of the e-learning course. This figure could deliver the reflective questions for consideration by the project team. This technique could be used in either an e-learning or a live virtual environment, but it may seem strange or impersonal when a live instructor is present.

❖ Have multiple teams work on the same project and have them present to each other, to compare approaches.

TIE: Action Plans

A popular end-of-training activity in many face-to-face and live virtual training classes, and to a limited extent, in e-learning courses, is the action plan. Participants make a list of how they plan to apply their learning. More detailed and sophisticated action planning tools include sharing the completed action plan with the participant's supervisor and other participants after training, listing obstacles that may interfere with completing the steps in the plan, target dates and milestones, and desired results. There are many different formats for action plans. A browser search on "action plan images" produces many different formats which can be used as models to develop specific action plans for different courses.

A trainer's focus tends to be on *where and when* in the training to use the action plan and on the design of the form itself. But what happens to the action plan after the training is over? Most are tossed away or left to gather dust, instead of being implemented. A few trainees may implement some items on their action plan, and an occasional trainee may put to use an entire comprehensive action plan, but frequent reminders and follow-ups by the trainer are necessary to ensure that more participants put more of their action plans into use.

Less is more when it comes to action items. An action plan that has more than seven or eight actions on it can be overwhelming and will decrease chances that any of the items will be completed. Three or four action items are ideal.

To use for e-learning

1. Develop an action plan form that is appropriate for the class. You can perform a simple browser search for "action plan images" to review various templates for action plans, and settle on one that is most suitable for your needs.

2. Toward the end of the training class, before the test (if there is one), provide the form for participants to complete. Depending on the authoring system capabilities, trainees may save the form to their hard drive and

complete them as instructed, or follow a link to an online form from which data can be captured to share with the participant's supervisor.

3. You may also integrate the action plan at various points in the training, perhaps at the end of each module. Show the master form on a slide and ask the participant to access their own copies of it and add their personal action items.

4. Criteria can be provided for selecting action items, so that participants' lists don't get too long and unwieldy. Ask them to write down only those action items that are given priority by their managers, needed for current work tasks, or most important for overall career goals.

5. Design a follow-up reinforcement strategy for the action plan. Options include:

   ❖ Email reminders (via the LMS) to the trainees to execute their plans, to share and discuss them with their supervisors, or to print and post them in a prominent place.

   ❖ A follow-up email with trainees' supervisors, prompting them to discuss the action plans with their employees.

   ❖ An email follow-up with the peer, coach, or mentor designated by each participant. Contact information for this person could be collected in the class registration form or via a separate email sent at the time of registration.

   ❖ If the action plans the participants submitted were captured via the LMS, return them to participants at designated after-training intervals: one week, three weeks, six weeks, and three months.

6. Require at least a certain number of action items to be completed before credit for the class is given. While this is more difficult to implement than simple reminders, requiring this level of accountability will strengthen motivation considerably.

Require at least a certain number of action items to be completed before credit for the class is given.

Adaptations for live virtual training

1. Post the action plan form in the virtual classroom or email it to participants before the training. Ask participants to save it to their hard drive where it can be easily accessed during training. Instruct them to jot down specific steps they will take after training to apply what they have learned. Tell them they will be reminded after class to follow through with the action items they listed.

2. If there are multiple sessions in the class, introduce the action plan in an early session and ask trainees to add items to their plans at the end of each session or at the conclusion of a particular learning point.

Downsides

This TIE may not be effective if:

❖ Follow up and reinforcement parts of the program are not implemented.

❖ Action plan reminders sent via email are ignored for various reasons.

Variations

❖ Participants complete the action plan at the beginning of the training—after learning the objectives—so that they identify how they will apply what they are about to learn. They can then revisit their action plans at the end of the training and revise as necessary.

❖ Instead of cutting less important action items from their lists, have participants prioritize them.

TIE: Application Checks

Sometimes participants understand right away how a particular skill or piece of knowledge can be applied to their jobs and sometimes they don't. For those situations when they don't, use application checks throughout the training. This technique was first used in face-to-face training. Index cards were placed at tables and participants were regularly prompted to jot a note to themselves on the cards about how they would apply what they were learning.

In an e-learning class or live virtual training, prompt participants at key points to reflect on how they will apply what they are learning.

To use for e-learning

1. Determine key points when application checks will be most appropriate: at the conclusion of a particular learning point, at a point when participants may question whether they can apply a skill or subset of a skill, at the end of a module, or before or after quiz questions. Customize each application check so it includes a key question or two related to a specific learning point or skill.

2. Consider using a graphic with each application check prompt so participants will be able to quickly recognize it each time it appears.

3. For maximum impact, the trainees should be directed to write responses to the application checks. Many authoring platforms include a note-taking feature that can be used for this. Direct participants to go to their notes, write their response to the application check, and then save or print it. Another option is to provide a digital form for note-taking, in which you can insert prompts, and instruct participants to save it to their hard drive or print it and then take handwritten notes.

4. Include a link to a discussion forum, learning community, or other on-line platform where the application check can be posted and discussed collectively by participants. Participating in this discussion could be made a requirement for class completion.

5. At the end of the course and in post-training communication with trainees and their managers, mention their application checks and encourage them to refer back to them.

Customize each application check so it includes a key question or two related to a specific learning point or skill.

Adaptations for live virtual training

1. Prepare the pop-up or slide with a recognizable graphic and insert it at predetermined points in the slides for the class. Mention with each application check the specific learning point, skill, or task, and ask the participant to think about how they will use it in their work. Consider customizing each application check so it includes a key question or two related to that specific learning point or skill.

2. Provide space for participants to write their responses to application checks in the handout or workbook pages that accompany the class.

3. Allow 30 to 60 seconds for participants to write or think about their responses.

4. If the platform allows, play music to time these application check periods. Doing this also reduces the tendency to want to "fill up the dead space" and shorten the time allowed.

5. You may be tempted to ask participants to "chat" their responses to the application checks, but remember that they will not be able to easily save records of their answers for future reference. A better choice is to provide a handout for them to take notes on.

6. You may also form breakout groups in which participants can share their responses to the application checks. Or provide a link to a discussion forum, learning community, or other online platform where the application check can be posted and discussed collectively by participants. In this case allow time in class (just a few minutes) for them to follow the link and post their responses. This activity could be combined with a break.

Downsides

This TIE may not be effective if:

❖ Application of the learning is obvious and participants do not need to be prompted to think about it.

❖ Application checks are inserted at points that disrupt the flow of the training.

❖ The discussion board, learning community, or other platform designated for discussing application checks actually diverts participants' attention from the training.

Variations

❖ Send application checks via email before and after a training event (or between sessions of a live virtual training class). Ask trainees to reflect on how they have applied (or will apply) specific learning points, tasks, or skills. Ask them to post their responses to a discussion board or in a reply email to the trainer, training coordinator, and their manager.

Figure 3-1. Application Check

© Carnes and Associates, Inc.

TIE: Do Not Disturb

Work environments lend themselves to constant communication among co-workers—through email, instant messages, phone calls, and in-person visits. Because learners most often participate in e-learning and live virtual training at their own desks, their learning is often interrupted by these kinds of communication. These interruptions disrupt concentration, increase time needed to learn material, reduce the quantity of what is learned, and result in lower levels of learning transfer.

Some interruptions are unavoidable and must take priority over an e-learning class or live virtual event. However, in many situations the co-workers who are sending an IM, text message, or email to a trainee are not aware they are interrupting a learning experience. And the learner may not realize how each interruption is affecting the quality and quantity of her learning, as well as how it is affecting her ability to apply what she has learned to her job.

Interruptions disrupt trainee concentration, increase time needed to learn the material, reduce the quantity and quality of what is learned, and result in lower levels of learning transfer.

Interruptions are not limited to other people. Often we are our own enemies when it comes to learning. Learners may not see the value of the training they are participating in and look for opportunities to focus on something else. Self-distractions are particularly tempting if the training is poorly designed with a seemingly never-ending progression of slides and little to no interaction. But even if the training is well designed, with lots of tools for learner engagement, trainees may find ways to distract themselves. Educating and motivating learners to reduce their interruptions will lead to better learning and transfer.

Figure 3-2. Do Not Disturb

© Carnes and Associates, Inc.

To use for e-learning

1. In the registration confirmation message, tell participants that they should plan to turn off their email notification, close all other applications and clear their electronic desktops, including instant messaging, when working on the class. Depending on the culture and expectations of the organization, consider asking them to create an automatic outgoing message in their email program notifying senders that they are unavailable for specific time periods. Send a copy to their managers.

2. Supply participants with a sign that says "Do Not Disturb: Training in Progress," (such as the one depicted in Figure 3-3) with instructions to print it and place it in a visible spot in their workspaces while they are taking an e-learning class.

3. In the beginning of the e-learning program, remind trainees that they should be in a quiet area, away from distractions. Direct them to turn off their cellphones and email notifications, and to close any applications they may be using. Include an explanation such as, "Interruptions

prolong the time it will take for you to complete this class, and your learning may not be optimal."

4. In the beginning of the e-learning program, include instructions on how to refocus on the class if they have been interrupted or have stopped for any other reason. They should plan to navigate back at least three to four slides from the place where they stopped. If they do not fully remember the material at this point, they should go back to the beginning of the module or class and pick up from there.

Figure 3-3. "Do Not Disturb" Sign

© Carnes and Associates, Inc.

Adaptations for live virtual training

1. Explore the virtual classroom platform technology to determine what features are available to reduce distractions. Some classrooms display a certain icon if a learner navigates away from the classroom or is otherwise inattentive. Other classrooms do not allow the learner to rejoin the classroom if they have navigated away unless they reaccess the link and reregister.

2. During training, monitor the attentiveness indicators the technology provides. Consider sending an instant message to inattentive trainees

offering to help catch them up and fill them in on what they missed. Doing this lets them know that their inattention has been noticed.

3.   Consider implementing a rule, announced at the beginning of class, that anyone who is inattentive for 10 minutes or more will not receive credit for the class.

Downsides

This TIE may not be effective if:

❖ The organizational attitude toward training is very "check the box."

❖ Managers and senior leaders expect employees to be available at all times, even during training.

TIE: Do Now

A "Do Now" activity is a short, individual activity that may serve several purposes simultaneously. In live virtual training, it can occupy trainees while roll is taken or other administrative duties are dispensed with. It can also be used at the beginning of an e-learning or live virtual module to reinforce learning from the previous module.

The "Do Now" activity can be used as an icebreaker, closing activity, or "homework" (between live virtual sessions), but it should take no more than three minutes. It should serve the dual purpose of making constructive use of otherwise dead time for the trainee, and providing quick opportunities to reinforce or apply the learning. Do not confuse a "Do Now" activity with an icebreaker question. This TIE asks the participant to do something, independently.

"Do Now" activities serve the dual purpose of making constructive use of otherwise dead time for the trainee, and providing quick opportunities to reinforce or apply the learning.

To use for e-learning

1. Refer to the learning objectives for a class, and then list activities the participant can do on their own in approximately three minutes, to introduce, reinforce, or apply one of the key learning concepts.

2. If each module of the training is loaded separately, provide a "Do Now" activity on the last screen of each module, that participants can do while they wait for the next module to load. For example, consider a "Do Now" activity in the context of a multiple-module e-learning course on ethics training. The first module covers common ethical dilemmas in a particular industry. The trainee takes the first module, passes the quiz. Before proceeding to the next module, a "Do Now" screen appears and

directs the trainee to conduct a browser search on a specified search term such as "ethical dilemmas in _____ industry," and to quickly scan the first article that comes up.

3. A unique "Do Now" graphic will help trainees recognize each "Do Now" activity.

Adaptations for live virtual training

1. Identify key points in the training that will be appropriate for a "Do Now" activity: a few minutes before the training begins, or as the trainer is preparing for the next phase of the training or pausing to address a problem.

2. When designing "Do Now" activities for the virtual classroom, keep in mind how the live virtual technology platform deals with participants navigating away from it. If participants must sign in all over again, do not use activities that require them to navigate away from the classroom.

3. You may refer to the "Do Now" activity at a later point in the training, but it is intended to be a stand-alone activity. Do not "process" the activity by leading participants in a lengthy discussion of it.

Downsides

This TIE may not be effective if:

❖ The trainer or e-learning designer makes it into a complex or interactive activity.

❖ It takes longer than five minutes.

❖ It takes the trainee away from the training module or classroom without an easy way to re-enter, or otherwise is not supported by the technology platform.

Variation

❖ Send "Do Now" activities via email to participants as supplements to the training. Most LMSs can be set up to do this automatically.

TIE: Feel-Felt-Found

This little technique is somewhat different from the other TIEs because it is not a process, product, or deliverable. It is just a simple technique to use in a variety of ways with trainees and their supervisors, to support several transfer-related goals.

The feel-felt-found technique is often used in sales to gently move people to a new way of thinking and to overcome concerns ("objections," in sales terminology). It has three parts. The first part involves empathizing with the other person's point of view. *I understand how you feel.* Stating this legitimizes the trainee's or manager's position. The second part indicates that others in the trainee's or manager's position have also felt this way; that their way of thinking is not unique, but is in fact common. The underlying meaning is that their situations or positions can change. *Others have felt this way.* The third part states that these other people changed their minds, did what was requested or recommended, and found that the outcome was positive. *What they found, however, was that after doing X, Y happened.*

This feel-felt-found sequence can be used several different ways to make learning stick:

❖ To support a "you can do it" attitude in the participant, which promotes self-confidence and self-efficacy. This attitude is strongly related to better transfer of training to the job.

❖ To encourage trainees' managers to have pre-training and post-training discussions, to provide opportunities to practice and use the new skills, to reduce interruptions during training, and to hold trainees accountable to use newly learned skills.

❖ To convince participants that the training will be useful to them in their jobs and careers.

To use for e-learning

1. At the beginning of an e-learning course, use three slides to increase trainee motivation, the belief that they can pass the class, and the conviction that the training will be useful to them.

2. For example, in a mandatory compliance class, the first slide would read: "You may be thinking that this class won't be useful to you and that you just want to get through it." The second slide would read, "Others have certainly felt this way." The third slide would read, "However, what other people have found is that the types of dilemmas we will be discussing in today's training come up more often than they thought, and the guidelines in this class have helped them take the lead in solving these kinds of problems." Use supporting graphics on each slide to add visual interest.

3. In pre-training and post-training communication with trainees' supervisors, use the feel-felt-found technique to overcome possible resistance to what is being requested. For example, in a pre-training email: "You may think that you don't have time to sit down and have a conversation with your employee about the training they are going to take. Other managers certainly have felt this way too. What they have found, though, is that the discussion took them only one to two minutes, and it helped them get a much better return on their investment in training their employee."

Adaptations for live virtual training

1. Use the real-time interactivity of virtual classrooms to your advantage. Address trainees' concerns in feel-felt-found language at the beginning of class.

2. Use a poll to introduce a feel-felt-found message. Trainees can select from options like, "I can see how this training will help me do my job better and advance my career"; "I am not sure how this training will help me do my job better and advance my career"; "I feel that this training will not make any difference in how I do my job or help my career." Follow up the poll with the feel-felt-found message.

Downsides

This TIE may not be effective if:

❖ It is clear how the training can be used and participants do not lack confidence or motivation.

❖ Managers are eager to do their part in supporting the training.

Variations

❖ Provide testimonials from others to strengthen the "found" portion of the message.

❖ Use the feel-felt-found message in the registration confirmation email to participants.

A feel-felt-found statement can be used to overcome objections or doubts participants may have about the training.

TIE: KISS—Keep It Simple or Supervised

In a research study of trainees who were learning PowerPoint, two variables were manipulated and assessed: learner control and the complexity of the material. The learners in the study were given varying degrees of control over which modules to take, when to take the training, and which activities to participate in. Some learners underwent a complex version of the training with many more concepts to learn while others underwent a simpler version with less material. Then transfer of the training content was measured. The results showed that transfer levels were much higher for the participants who took the less complex version of the training, and for those who had lower levels of control. (The word "supervised" is used in the title here to represent lower levels of learner control.)

While it is believed that most learners prefer higher levels of control over their learning, if the learning content is complex then they are probably not learning and applying it very well—or as well as they would be if their training efforts were more supervised. The study concluded that the more complex the material, the more important it is to provide a learning experience in which the learner does not have control over the sequence, the time spent on the material, and other variables often offered in self-paced e-learning classes.

If the learning content is complex, it is important for the trainer to exert more control over the learning experience so that he is assured the participants are learning and applying the content as intended.

Despite what a subject matter expert may want or expect, the more simple and straightforward the training content, the more likely it is to be learned and applied. This doesn't mean to "dumb down" the material, but rather deliver it at a reasonable rate. Additional modules may need to be added in order to thoroughly explain a concept and slow the learner's pace. Consider excluding the "nice to know" material (or provide it as an appendix, a "Did You Know?" segment, or other ancillary feature that clearly distinguishes it from the "need to know" content).

To use for e-learning

1. Review the learning material and evaluate its complexity. The quickest, easiest way to do this is to count the number of concepts presented. The more concepts presented per module, the more complex the content.

2. Simplify the content by either reducing the number of concepts presented or adding additional modules so that the number of concepts per module is lower. Aim for three to five concepts per module.

3. Clearly distinguish the "need to know" concepts from the "nice to know" concepts, by linking to additional information, including optional modules, or by presenting a "Nice to Know" feature in various screens or links that learners can view if interested.

4. Employ features of the e-learning platform that reduce learner control, such as requiring that a certain amount of time be spent on each screen or activity (most authoring software has this capability) and dictating the order in which the modules must be taken.

5. Test participants rigorously on the learning content, require a high score to pass the test, and do not allow the learner to advance to the next module until they pass the previous one.

Adaptations for live virtual training

1. Add an additional virtual training session to cover advanced concepts, for those who are interested in them or are required to learn them. This training session should be offered only to those who have demonstrated mastery of the basic content.

2. Use the features of the virtual classroom to exert more control over the learner experience. Monitor their attentiveness and engage individuals

directly if necessary. Form breakout groups to discuss any concepts that deserve extra explanation.

3. Test participants on the material. Many virtual training platforms do not have testing features so it may be necessary to use or adapt quiz software and link it to the LMS for this purpose.

Downsides

This TIE may not be effective if:

* The learners begin the class with very different levels of prior knowledge.

* Trainee satisfaction and happiness is more important than their learning and application of the material.

TIE: A Little Help From Friends

One of the reasons frequently given for why face-to-face classes will never become obsolete is the opportunities for interaction that they present. Many trainees appreciate and benefit from the support and feedback of their peers, as well as learn from listening to the questions and answers they voice in class.

Participants with high transfer rates had talked with colleagues before taking the training, learning from them how the class would help them with their jobs, things to watch out for, and other tips for learning and using the information and skills.

Interaction and support from peers need not be limited to fellow participants, however. A research study found that participants with high transfer rates had talked with colleagues before taking the training, learning from them how the class would help them with their jobs, things to watch out for, and other tips for learning and using the information and skills. Another study found that trainees who were paired up with peers who had previously taken the training received valuable advice and assistance from them, which enabled the trainees to put the knowledge to use more easily.

Support also need not be limited to those with peers who had taken the training previously. Individuals who undertake a challenge such as losing weight or running a marathon frequently enlist the support of nonparticipating friends to cheer them on. Why not encourage participants to do the same thing, particularly if the learning will be lengthy, especially challenging, or difficult to complete in other ways? The focus of this TIE is this kind of supportive relationship, regardless of the source or the medium for the interaction.

To use for e-learning

1. At the beginning of the training, suggest to the participants that they enlist the support and company of their peers for this journey. Identify some criteria to guide their choosing of this friend (or friends):

   ❖ someone who will take an interest in their learning and development

   ❖ someone they interact with regularly—or would like to interact with regularly

   ❖ a family member or close personal friend

   ❖ a co-worker who has similar career goals in mind, or has taken similar training.

2. Make suggestions on what kinds of support they should ask of this person. Possibilities include progress reports, verbal encouragement, problem-solving assistance, simply listening, or perhaps even freeing up the trainee's time by temporarily taking on their personal or work responsibilities.

3. Provide cues throughout the program for the participant to check in with their friend. While not necessary, it may be useful to also provide some structure such as:

   ❖ Discuss with your friend three things that you have learned in this module.

   ❖ Tell your friend the hardest thing about applying this step in the process.

   ❖ Discuss with your friend what they thought and how they felt when they were tackling this part of the training.

Adaptations for live virtual training

1. In later sessions, perhaps as an icebreaker, ask participants to share any valuable advice or feedback provided by their friend.

2. Invite the friends to participate in a closing activity or final training session and acknowledge their role.

Downsides

This TIE may not be effective if:

* The training is not very challenging for the participant, so that outside support is superfluous.

* The trainee's natural style is to work independently, so that sharing and getting support from friends is contrary to his nature.

* The training is a single, live virtual class.

Variations

* Assign "buddies" who are fellow participants in the training. Define their roles, providing opportunities, structured questions, or assignments to help them connect and interact in between training sessions. In self-paced e-learning, use the LMS to pair people who are taking the class at the same time.

TIE: Live Pilot

Unreliable technology is a significant barrier to learning transfer. Many times the e-learning developer is notified about an issue, fixes the problem, and the learner re-engages and finishes the class. Other times, estimated to be numerous, the learner abandons the class, or if it is possible, finds a way to finish the class while avoiding key parts where technical problems have occurred.

What may work well in the developer's environment may have bugs and glitches when it is run in the learner's (or instructor's) environment, due to different plug-ins, rules, settings, and hardware, so that the user experience varies for each participant. It can be maddeningly difficult to separate program bugs and technology platform issues from issues in the learner's own technical environment. Also, pressure to release the program may interfere with final testing efforts that ensure all aspects of the class are working properly. It is possible (and more time-efficient) to field test e-learning classes and live virtual training in a face-to-face classroom.

Advantages of this approach include:

* The trainer (who may or may not be the developer) can monitor how trainees interact with the material, addressing questions or confusion about the program on the spot.

* Bugs in the program can be identified and steps can be taken to correct them more quickly and easily than in a virtual environment, where learners are separated by distance and issues with their own systems.

* The trainer is able to assess the time learners take to complete the program.

---

*Program bugs can be identified and corrected more quickly
and easily during the live pilot, when users and trainers
are physically gathered, than in a virtual launch.*

There are a few disadvantages as well:

❖ Learners who have had to travel across town or several buildings may be unhappy, believing they could have taken the class at their desks.

❖ Launching in a face-to-face classroom may not identify all technical issues in learners' environments that may cause problems.

❖ Trainees who take the class after it has become completely virtual may expect or want the face-to-face experience.

To use for e-learning

1. Draft modules as usual, perhaps eliminating the final debugging step.

2. Schedule a face-to-face training class in a computer classroom or ask participants to bring their own laptops. Ideally the classroom trainer would also be the e-learning developer, but any trainer who is knowledgeable about the content and familiar with the authoring application will be able to conduct the class.

3. If some but not all of the e-learning modules are completed, blend the learning, integrating e-learning modules with face-to-face instruction.

4. Observe and solicit feedback from participants.

5. Restrict questions and discussion on content to specified times to provide the best environment to assess the e-learning technology. Allow trainees to work on their own at the computers during most of the class time.

6. At the end of the training, conduct a discussion about the learner's experience with the training. Use this information to make adjustments to the e-learning.

Adaptations for live virtual training

1. Draft the training in the usual way, developing visuals and activities that will be used in a virtual classroom.

2. Participants should connect to the virtual classroom in the usual way, but should be seated in the face-to-face classroom. They should turn their

volume down or off, listen to the live instructor, and rely on the virtual classroom for visuals only. (This may seem awkward at first, especially if participants are facing away from the front of the room, but after a few minutes they will adjust.)

Downsides

This TIE may not be effective if:

❖ The training is bug-free and learners' technical environments are well known and not problematic.

❖ Participants are widely dispersed geographically.

Variations

❖ Blend an e-learning class with live virtual training. Participants in this case are connected via the virtual training platform as they participate in e-learning modules. While the trainer's ability to monitor trainees is more limited than in a face-to-face environment, some monitoring of learner activity is possible through the virtual classroom technology. This option would work best when some but not all of the modules are in e-learning format, and when learners are dispersed geographically and not available for a live launch.

❖ Design a class for both e-learning and instructor-led (face-to-face) presentations. Some settings in the e-learning version will probably need to be adjusted in this case. If the instructor-led program will be projected or shown on a monitor larger than the typical workstation, the screen size will probably need to be increased. Branching features used in the e-learning program will be more difficult, if not impossible, to use for an instructor-led program.

TIE: Manager Module

In the early years of workplace learning it was not unusual to require manager involvement in particular training programs. Trainees' managers were either required to attend the same training as their employees, or undergo a separate, shorter training created just for them. This executive version covered key points of the training in less detail, and usually did not include practice or other activities.

Today's technologies provide easy, time-efficient opportunities to include managers. No need to travel to a face-to-face class anymore. Use LMSs to track manager participation and limit employee access to a course until their manager has taken the corresponding module.

To use for e-learning

1. Develop the participant version of the training first. Then answer the following questions:

    ❖ What aspects of this training will need to be reinforced or modeled by their supervisor?

    ❖ Which parts of the training may be contrary to how things are being done on the job, by the manager, by other employees, or by the participants in this training?

2. Use your answers to the questions above to develop learning objectives for the manager module. When designing it, keep in mind that this training should be significantly shorter than the participant training.

3. Plan to cover these key points about how managers should support their employees' learning application:

    ❖ Provide frequent opportunities for employees to use what they have learned.

    ❖ Communicate with each trainee after the training to go over what he learned and how he can apply it.

    ❖ Express confidence in their ability to apply their learning.

4. The length of this manager module will be determined to some extent by the content of the participant training, but make every effort to keep it short. The longer the training, the more challenging it will probably be to get managers to take it. A good rule of thumb is to make manager training shorter than participant training by 75 percent.

5. Determine whether to require a manager's participation prior to accepting registrations from any of their employees. If their participation is to be voluntary, set up the LMS so that each time an employee registers for this class, their manager receives an invitation and a link to register (until they take it).

A good rule of thumb is to make manager training shorter than participant training by 75 percent.

Adaptation for live virtual training

1. Consider recording the first presentation of the manager module so that it can be accessed on demand by managers if they desire.

Downsides

This TIE may not be effective if:

* Senior leadership does not support manager participation in the manager module.

* Participants have no motivation to encourage their manager to take the module. (Requiring that managers complete their module before participants can register—or receive credit for—their module will solve this.)

* The module contains so much information or takes so long that managers are not willing to spend time on it.

Variations

* Offer a manager module that focuses on how to support employee training in general, without referring to content in specific training.

TIE: Note to Self

This TIE is an adaptation of a closing activity used by many facilitators in face-to-face training. At the conclusion of the training, participants are handed a blank sheet of paper and an envelope, and are asked to reflect on what they learned in the training and how they plan to use it. When they finish their letter, they address the envelope to themselves and seal it. The trainer collects the envelopes. At a later time, usually three to six weeks after the training, the trainer mails the envelopes to trainees. Many trainees have reported that they were surprised to receive letters from themselves, having forgotten they wrote them in class. This surprise factor and the contents of their letters serve as reminders and motivators to apply what they learned.

Learners' "notes to self" remind them to apply what they learned after the training is over.

Adapting this activity to e-learning and live virtual training is easy. Email takes the place of paper and envelope. The purpose and the outcome remain the same: Participants write personalized reminders to themselves to apply their learning to their jobs. In addition, technology provides opportunities to share their thoughts with their managers, peers, or others who can support them as they apply their learning.

To use for e-learning

1. At the end of the course, following the final summary and prior to a quiz or exam, prompt trainees to write summaries of what they have learned and a few ways they plan to apply it. Ask them to consider any barriers they might encounter and how they can overcome them. Provide a link for this to a form or the notes section of the e-learning program.

2. Instruct trainees to send this summary to themselves, using the "send later" feature of their email program to delay their receiving the message

until the appropriate time. Set up the LMS to send out emails one to three weeks after training to remind participants to review their "notes to self."

Downsides

This TIE may not be effective if:

❖ Trainees aren't prompted to review their notes to themselves one to three weeks after training.

Variations

❖ Ask participants to copy their manager (or a supportive peer) on emails to themselves, as added reinforcement.

❖ Prompt participants to post a note in their calendar or task feature of their email program for one to three weeks after they complete the class, reminding themselves what they have learned and how they will apply it.

TIE: Picture This

Psychologists and advertisers have known for a long time that a picture is worth a thousand words. An effective way to prompt people to take action is to show them a picture that holds some meaning for them. Pictures can be especially useful in motivating trainees to transfer their learning. A recent training experiment found that when trainees were shown photos of a person winning a race along with written instructions on how to sell their product, their sales were significantly higher than those who were given written instructions alone.

Using a picture to illustrate how to perform a skill is helpful, of course. Planting a motivational suggestion is a bit different. In this TIE, the motivational suggestion is to apply the newly learned skill to the job.

An effective way to prompt people to take action is to show them a picture that holds some meaning for them.

To use in e-learning

1. Find a photo that depicts success. Obvious choices would be someone winning a race, receiving an award, or cheering. Another choice might be a photo of someone successfully performing the targeted skills on the job; of course, this could be more difficult to procure and there is no research to support this type of photo's effect on learners. If searching the web for images, use terms such as "success," "winning," and "champion." If you use images sourced from the web, be sure to respect copyrights. Creative Commons is currently a great site to use for finding licensed content and images (*www.creativecommons.org*). Also, portable devices make it very easy to take photographs that lend a personalized touch to the training, which participants may find more engaging than generic images procured from the web.

2. Use the success photo as background for an "action transfer slide." If the technology does not allow using the photo as background, include the photo on the slide in the usual way photos are placed.

Downside

This TIE may not be effective if:

❖ The success photo chosen is not appropriate for a particular trainee group. For example, the success photo depicts a person in a business suit climbing a ladder and the trainee group consists of nurses.

Variations

❖ Have posters made of the photos with reminders. Send them to participants and encourage them to post them in their cubicles or in common work areas where large numbers of trainees have completed the training.

❖ Use the photo as the background in the body of an after-training email reminder to use what they learned.

❖ Email the photo with action item reminders on it to participants after the training. Encourage them to install it as desktop wallpaper or as a screen-saver for 30 to 60 days to help cement their new skills.

TIE: Pop-Up Reflections

The fact that the learner controls his learning experience can be both a blessing and a curse. While the benefits of learner control in self-paced e-learning and live virtual training are many, there is the constant risk of trainees moving through the screens too quickly, distracting themselves by responding to emails, phone calls, and other interruptions, and otherwise failing to focus on the learning.

Several studies have found that when learners were prompted to reflect on what they were doing—and not doing—during their learning experience, their completion rates were up to 30 percent higher, and their test scores were also higher. One study also found that pop-up messaging (in the form of emails) after training that prompted participants to use what they learned resulted in more transfer.

When learners are prompted to reflect on their progress through training sessions, their completion rates, test scores, and transfer levels are higher.

To use for e-learning

1. Review each learning module and try to identify points—due to length or content—at which learners might be most likely to lose attention.

2. Develop pop-up reflection questions. You can use general questions that prompt learners to reflect on their learning, or ask content-specific questions such as:

   ❖ Do I understand these five pointers for network programming?

   ❖ Once I am back on the job, will I be able to recall this information on dealing effectively with conflict?

   ❖ How will I use these techniques to overcome objections in my sales calls?

❖ Which of my internal customers will need to know about this change in procedure?

❖ What are some specific ways that I can apply what I am learning?

Figure 3-4. Pop-Up Reflection Questions (General)

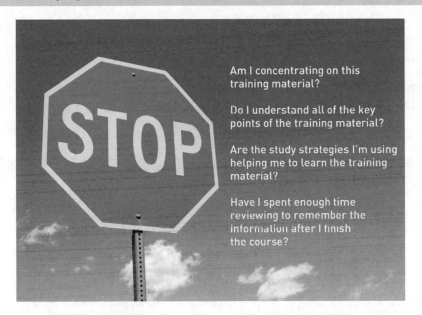

3. Program the reflection questions to pop up at the appropriate points and remain on the screen for 10 to 15 seconds. If pop-ups are not possible, simply insert a screen with the reflection questions at chosen points in the program.

Adaptations for live virtual training

1. Insert pop-up reflection questions into the slides: approximately three to five of them per hour of training, when trainees might be likely to lose attention.

2. When pop-up reflections appear, make sure to allow a short pause in which participants can consider the questions on the slide. Do not talk or play music during this time. Conclude with a simple "thank you."

Downsides

This TIE may not be effective if:

❖ The live virtual trainer feels the need to keep talking during the pop-up.

❖ The pop-up messages are in the form of statements ("do this") rather than in the language of self-reflection.

Variations

❖ Send email "pop-up" questions after training, prompting participants to self-monitor their post-training behavior and skill use. Most LMSs can be set up to automatically send a series of emails at designated intervals post-training.

Figure 3-5. Pop-Up Reflection Questions (Content-Specific)

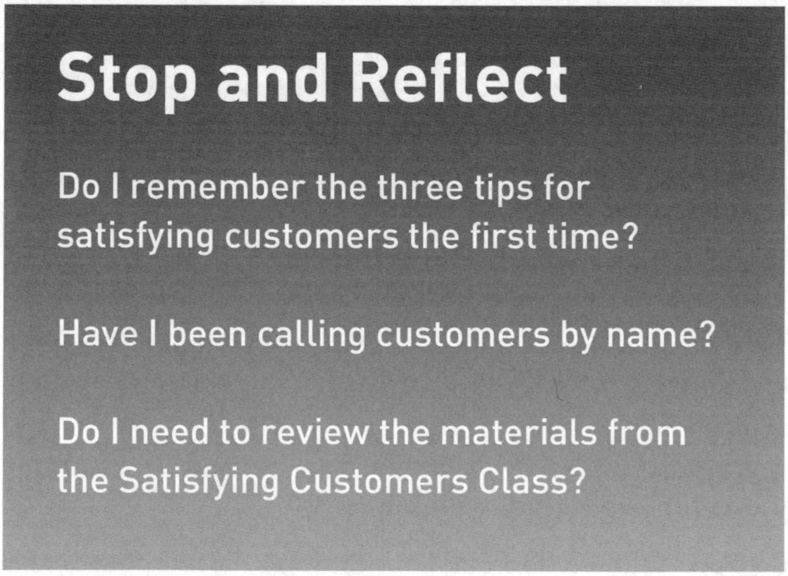

Stop and Reflect

Do I remember the three tips for satisfying customers the first time?

Have I been calling customers by name?

Do I need to review the materials from the Satisfying Customers Class?

TIE: QR Codes

Quick Response Codes are becoming increasingly popular in consumer advertising. They contain a type of two-dimensional code that, when read by a device such as a smartphone or tablet, provides immediate access to a site with more information about a product or service.

QR codes can be used to support training transfer in several different ways, all of which make use of a trainee's mobile device and time away from her computer. For example, when a trainee needs to access the information that is linked to the QR code, she can simply scan the code with her mobile device to reveal information linked to the training: step-by-step instructions, video clips, diagrams, additional instructions. Having additional tools and information at trainees' disposal provides opportunities to help them build their self-confidence and efficacy, understand how the training can be used in their jobs, reduce distractions during training, and provide reinforcement of the learning material. QR codes can be the means to implement many of the TIEs in this book, including Do Now, Sticky Kit for Managers, A Little Help from Friends, Threaded Discussions, Action Learning, and Sticky Blog.

QR codes can be used to support training transfer in several different ways, all of which make use of a trainee's mobile device and time away from her computer. When a trainee needs to access the information that is linked to the QR code, she can simply scan the code with her mobile device to reveal information linked to the training.

Making a QR code is easy. There are websites that allow you to create QR codes for free, while others charge a small fee or offer a subscription plan. Input your data—typically a URL or a small bit of text—and download the QR image, which can then be pasted into class materials, an email, or any other document in much the same way as a photo. QR codes can hold just over 4,000 alpha-numeric characters; however, keep in mind that storage space differs for other types of data you may wish to attach to the QR code (text messages can usually include no more than 160 characters).

To read the QR code, first install the free QR reading app on a smartphone, tablet, or other portable device. Then hold the device in front of the code until it "locks in," and the information is transferred to the device where it can be accessed.

To use with e-learning and live virtual training

1. Identify or create pre-training messages, URLs, video segments, or other resources that will prepare trainees for the training, such as preparatory information, instructions for practice, can-do motivational messages, reinforcement techniques, and short quizzes or exercises that can be completed using a mobile device.

2. Because trainees are likely to access their mobile devices when they are not at their workspaces but rather while they're on the go, make activities short.

3. Access the QR code generator site. Note that free sites have limited capabilities. Check with your marketing or advertising department to see if they have a subscription for more sophisticated QR code features. Enter the information to be contained in the code and download it in seconds.

4. Paste the QR code into a pre-class or post-class email, or into class slides, with instructions to view it on their portable device when they have a "quick minute."

5. Keep in mind that the LMS may not be able to track quiz scores or activity participation when learning materials are accessed this way.

Downsides

This TIE may not be effective if:

❖ It is necessary to document all training participation and the LMS is unable to track access through QR codes.

❖ Trainees do not have mobile devices.

❖ The training contains proprietary or confidential information for which higher measures of security are necessary.

Variation

❖ Display the QR code on a slide in the live virtual training class. Ask participants to pass their mobile devices over their screens to access supplemental information, an activity, or quiz.

Figure 3-6. QR Code

TIE: Sticky Blog

A blog is a great way to reinforce learning, provide information, stimulate trainees, encourage accountability, and make e-learning and live virtual classes stick. Blogs provide online space for posting content that includes links to other sites, images, and other resources, and is followed by chronologically ordered comments from readers. The "sticky blog" should be specific to a particular class or group of classes so the information and recommended resources are appropriate.

Use a sticky blog before training to provide motivation to learn. Help the trainees visualize how they will be able to do their jobs more easily, safely, and effectively with the skills and information they are about to learn. Pre-training sticky blog posts can also be used to help the trainee motivate their manager to provide freedom from interruptions while they are taking the training, or to perform requested pre-training tasks. Blog posts can also be used to boost trainees' belief in their ability to learn the content and apply it back on the job.

Blog posts to be viewed during the training can provide additional examples, practice exercises, answers to frequently asked questions, and other material that may not fit in the course itself due to time or space limitations. Content that perhaps had to be cut from the e-learning or live virtual training design is a good candidate for blog material. A blog also provides an opportunity for participants to connect with the trainer during a self-paced e-learning class. A frequent complaint learners have about e-learning courses is that there isn't anybody to answer questions or provide further explanations as needed, as there would be in a live class. A blog can provide this connection. The blog can also be used to stage a "virtual field trip" with photos or videos.

Blog posts can provide additional information such as examples, practice exercises, answers to frequently asked questions, and other material that may not fit in the course itself due to time or space limitations.

Use a sticky blog after training to post additional information, such as examples, case studies, exercises, and tips trainees can use to apply their learning. Invite trainees to share a behavior they changed, a success they experienced, an obstacle they overcame, or a process they challenged as they began using what they learned in the class. Include suggestions for trainees' managers on how to provide post-training support.

A blog can be a static repository of information or it can be a moderated, dynamic place. If the blog is moderated, trainees could post questions and receive answers from the instructor or subject matter experts. It can also be a forum in which to post and discuss assignments and class projects. Trainees can be asked—or required—to post their answers to content-specific questions or prompts from the trainer.

A blog has several advantages over other social media outlets, such as a microblog (see the Sticky Microblog TIE) or a learning community. It can invite more reflection, more thoughtful and insightful comments, and more analysis and critical thinking from both trainer and participant. Also, unlike other social media tools, it can be archived for later reference and use.

To use with e-learning

1. Visualize how the blog should be used by learners.

    ❖ What information, tips, or guidance would be good for trainees to have prior to taking this class? Posting helpful materials will drive traffic to the blog and also save class time.

    ❖ What additional information, resources, links, videos, and photos would supplement the course content but can't be included in class due to time limitations?

    ❖ What assignments would enhance trainees' learning and application, and how could these be included in a blog? Possible options include posting an opinion to spark discussion or a structured debate, posting case studies, staging a virtual field trip, featuring learners' reactions to assigned readings, valuable advice, or encouraging stories.

    ❖ Will learners be required to participate in the discussions hosted on the blog?

2. Find a hosting platform for the blog. Consult the IT department before doing this. If the blog content is sensitive or based on proprietary information, it will need to be behind the company firewall. Many LMSs and other platforms that operate behind firewalls, such as SharePoint, have blog capabilities. Otherwise, developer-hosted blogs are probably the best choice. Look in the URL of your favorite professional blogs to see who hosts them, or do a browser search on "blog hosting." There are many free hosting plans available.

3. Determine which permissions to use, if any. Who can view the blog? Will comments need to be approved by someone before they can be posted? If participants will be expected or required to submit posts, make sure to adjust the permissions so that their comments can be published without moderator approval.

4. Develop content for the blog. The nice thing about a blog is that it doesn't have to be as tightly organized as an e-learning course needs to be. Compose entries as if writing an email. Some entries may be a few lines, while others may be longer. Shorter is usually better. Be sure to include links to other online resources. An occasional photo adds to the visual landscape. Focus on success stories, vignettes, examples, and videos that discuss how to successfully apply the skills. Invite trainees to post assignments to the blog. Make sure to create separate entries for each assignment to keep the blog organized so that it is easier to follow and find posts.

5. Develop accountabilities and motivators to drive learners to the blog. For example, ask trainees to post a tip, an example, or something to watch out for. You can also ask trainees to post photos of themselves that are somehow related to the training (using certain equipment, at their consoles, performing the skill being taught). Decide whether their participation will be required for course completion or will be optional.

6. Include links to the blog in multiple places: in the registration email if participants should visit the blog before class, on a slide or two during the class, in the chat field, and in a follow-up email.

7. Be sure to revisit the blog occasionally even if it is a static blog. Check the links to be sure they are still active and lead to the intended content. Add resources, news, videos, vignettes, and so forth to keep the blog current.

Adaptations for live virtual training

1. Use the blog for between-session or after-session assignments to enhance trainees' learning and application. Have them post their opinions, share experiences doing a practice assignment, engage in a debate (assign sides), review case studies, take a virtual field trip, or describe their reactions to assigned readings, lessons learned, and success stories.

2. Set up two deadlines: first, for posting entries, and second, for reading them.

3. Discuss reactions to blog posts in the live virtual session (via chat or breakout groups).

4. Learners will probably be more comfortable posting to a blog that is limited to their classmates, so establish a new blog for each class. Consider this as well when establishing permissions as to who can view the blog.

Downsides

This TIE may not be effective if:

❖ The training content is relatively straightforward so that additional resources and information are not really necessary.

❖ The assignments or other dynamic content can be more easily accomplished or accessed in other ways.

Variations

❖ Develop a general blog which is not class-specific. Include tips for having a successful self-paced e-learning or live virtual class experience, such as how and where to take notes, how and when to review material, how to avoid interruptions and distractions, and so forth. Send a link to this blog each time someone registers for a class.

❖ Develop a general blog for managers on how to support an employee during training. Include tips such as how to identify opportunities for them to use their new skills, how to hold a short debriefing session after training is completed, and how to arrange for employees' usual responsibilities to be covered while they are in class. Send a link to the blog with the registration confirmation from the LMS or with the course completion email.

TIE: Sticky Heat Map

A heat map is a graphic representation of data in which the values are represented as different shades of colors. There are many different types of heat maps, including two-dimensional and three-dimensional representations, clusters, and bar graphs. A heat map can be used in training evaluation to display satisfaction with various aspects of the training (level 1), results of demonstrations or tests of learning (level 2), results of demonstrations or tests of transfer (level 3), and results of various impact indicators (level 4).

The heat map can also be used as a feedback mechanism to help training stick. Share the map with managers of trainees to help them identify areas they need to coach, reinforce training content, or provide practice opportunities. Share the map with trainees so they understand the areas they are doing well and the areas they need to better apply their training. The heat map can also display how various departments, units, or divisions compare with one another in how skills are applied. This comparison may spark healthy competition, which in turn may lead to better transfer.

> *Share the heat map with managers of trainees to help them identify areas where their employees need coaching, reinforcement of learning content, and practice opportunities.*

Data is essential to make a heat map but it does not need to be complicated, and collecting it does not need to be time-consuming. Over 95 percent of organizations collect level 1 evaluation data immediately after training. Consider adding a few questions about the trainees' intentions to use the learning in their jobs, in addition to gathering information on satisfaction ratings. Studies have found that intent to transfer is a reasonably good predictor of actual transfer. If trainees take level 2 end-of-module and end-of-class quizzes, the collective data on quiz scores can be shared with managers. This is also a good opportunity to review the quiz questions against the objectives to be sure that the quizzes are accurate tests of the material.

Fewer than 30 percent of organizations do any level 3 evaluation of transfer. It is easy to see why. Determining whether and how much of the training is used on the job can be difficult and time-consuming. A simple approach, however, involves asking whether trainees are using a particular skill that they learned in training on the job, and if so, how? Their answers can be collected quite easily using LMS survey software or survey software readily available on the Internet. Segment the information by department, group, or division to make the feedback more meaningful. Many managers will tend to discount data by saying in response to less-than-satisfactory data: "That may be true for *some* people in *some* divisions, but not in mine."

Create a heat map with spreadsheet software such as Excel by using the conditional formatting feature to color code the respective boxes. Use green for good scores, yellow for not-so-good, and red for bad, or needs attention.

To use with e-learning

1. Determine the key skills and behaviors covered in training that participants will be expected to use in their jobs. These may vary by department or work unit, but there should be a close relationship with the learning objectives for the training. If there is not, review and revise the learning objectives (see the Sticky Objectives TIE).

2. Decide on the purpose(s) of the heat map, for example:

   ❖ To motivate managers to take a more active role in post-training activities?

   ❖ To provide a comparison of training transfer across departments and divisions?

   ❖ To motivate participants to use more of what they have learned?

   ❖ To generate positive competition among departments and divisions?

3. Develop a few survey questions to capture the needed information for the specific purpose. The survey questions can be included in the end-of-class or end-of-module quiz, or a separate survey can be created.

4. Before you send out the survey, determine which software you will use to display the heat map.

5. Set up the LMS to automatically send the survey when a participant completes the training. If possible, the LMS or heat map software could automatically add in individual participant information as surveys are completed. This will take some initial set-up time but it will pay off if a large number of participants take the class. When enough survey responses have been received (follow-up reminders may be necessary), export the data to the spreadsheet using the export tool in the survey software.

6. Once results have been imported into a spreadsheet, create the heat map using the conditional formatting tool. Be sure to use these time-tested color schemes:

   ❖ Green—Good

   ❖ Yellow—Caution

   ❖ Red—Needs remedying

7. Share the heat map with those who should see it: trainees, managers, senior leadership. Use it to introduce after-training reinforcement strategies such as coaching, providing opportunities to practice, and peer support.

Adaptations for live virtual training

1. The polling feature in most live virtual technology platforms provides additional opportunity to gather information. Investigate this feature to see if the data from polls can be exported into a spreadsheet.

Variations

❖ Use the heat map concept for needs assessment, using the color coding to identify the most critical needs.

❖ Automate heat map creation by programming the LMS to automatically export data into the spreadsheet software, which has been set up to create the heat map.

❖ Try out specialized heat map software. Check out the latest ones by doing a browser search on "heat map software."

Figure 3-7. Sticky Heat Map

	Unit 1	Unit 2	Unit 3	Unit 4	Unit 5	Unit 6	Total
Objective 1: Are you using it?	72%	63%	88%	45%	57%	92%	70%
Using it w/customers?	40%	38%	51%	20%	23%	74%	41%
Using it w/employees?	67%	62%	70%	31%	51%	68%	58%
Objective 2: Are you using it?	74%	61%	92%	78%	68%	88%	77%
Using it w/customers?	44%	36%	82%	70%	33%	72%	56%
Using it w/employees?	58%	60%	70%	31%	48%	63%	55%
Objective 3: Are you using it?	21%	64%	53%	47%	50%	70%	51%
Using it w/customers?	17%	40%	51%	24%	33%	74%	40%
Using it w/employees?	20%	61%	40%	32%	48%	67%	45%
Objective 4: Are you using it?	68%	80%	84%	40%	91%	70%	72%
Using it w/customers?	51%	72%	74%	21%	85%	74%	63%
Using it w/employees?	22%	67%	68%	30%	57%	67%	52%

This is an example of a heat map that compares application, objective by objective, of a relationship management training program across six business units. The darkest shaded areas are red (need remedying), the moderately shaded areas are yellow (caution), and the least shaded areas are green (good).

© Carnes and Associates, Inc.

TIE: Sticky Kit for Managers

Marketing experts know that packaging makes a difference in how well a product sells. Selling managers on ways to support their employees' learning can be packaged too. Because managers have different styles of working with their employees, and because employees' job roles, physical locations, and other factors also make a difference in how a manager and employee interact, a Sticky Kit provides different ways for managers to assist their employees with the application of what has been learned in training.

A Sticky Kit can be prepared for each training program, or a more general one can be used that will apply to most e-learning or live virtual training programs. It can include a variety of tools for a manager to use, such as:

❖ briefing/debriefing key points

❖ meeting/contact tracking sheet

❖ training content overview and objectives—in text or video formats

❖ planning sheet for after-training practice and use of the new skills

❖ suggestions for reducing interruptions while training

❖ key points to communicate to fellow employees to enlist their support

❖ brief "sample" of the e-learning or previously recorded live virtual training session

❖ suggested case studies for discussion with trainees.

Providing managers with these options takes into account their different ways of working with their employees. It is also a good psychological move because it doesn't send a "do it this way or else" message, which often makes managers more resistant to trainers' requests.

Sticky Kits provide different ways for managers to assist their employees with the application of what has been learned in training.

Figure 3-8. Sample Email to Manager

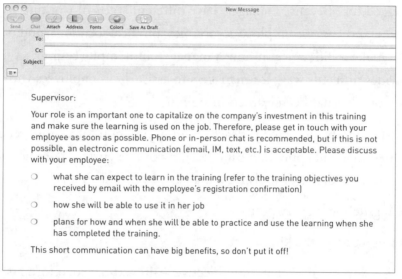

Supervisor:

Your role is an important one to capitalize on the company's investment in this training and make sure the learning is used on the job. Therefore, please get in touch with your employee as soon as possible. Phone or in-person chat is recommended, but if this is not possible, an electronic communication (email, IM, text, etc.) is acceptable. Please discuss with your employee:

○ what she can expect to learn in the training (refer to the training objectives you received by email with the employee's registration confirmation)

○ how she will be able to use it in her job

○ plans for how and when she will be able to practice and use the learning when she has completed the training.

This short communication can have big benefits, so don't put it off!

© Carnes and Associates, Inc.

To use with e-learning and live virtual training

1. Decide whether to use a more general Sticky Kit, or one that is designed for a specific class requiring higher levels of manager involvement. While it may be easier to prepare only one kit, managers may get tired of seeing this same kit, especially if they have many reports. Also, the content and nature of particular training classes may be a fit for some manager tools but not others.

2. Choose an attractive cover and a template that can be used with the various components. Remember, packaging helps sell the product. In most cases the Sticky Kit will be electronic, although a hard copy kit and forms may work better in some settings. Use the company logo, graphics or photos from the company website and intranet, or photos and graphics

3. related to the subject area. You can also repurpose graphics or photos from the e-learning program or slides from the live virtual training.

4. Develop the Sticky Kit. Make an effort to provide a variety of media for the supervisor to choose from: video, podcast, electronic forms, print-and-write forms, and so forth.

5. Link the Sticky Kit to the LMS registration process, if possible. A participant's registration confirmation email to the manager could include a heads-up comment that they will receive the Sticky Kit within so many days. While the Sticky Kit could be attached to the registration confirmation email, it is more likely to be overlooked when it is sent at the same time.

6. Follow up with managers to determine which items in the kit are being used most often. A simple survey tool can be used for this. This follow-up will also serve as a reminder for them to use the kit.

Downsides

This TIE may not be effective if:

❖ Supervisors do not have a clear understanding of their role in transferring training to the job. (Include information in the Sticky Kit to educate them.)

❖ The Sticky Kit components are not appealing or user-friendly.

❖ The Sticky Kit gets "lost in the shuffle" of a manager's workload. (Find a way to make it stand out.)

Variations

❖ Send the various Sticky Kit components to managers one at a time.

❖ Make managers accountable for completing one to two items in the kit by requesting that the completed forms be returned to the training department, to the course developer, or to their manager.

❖ Use interactive online tools rather than static word processing or spreadsheet documents. When supervisors complete these kinds of tools they can be tracked, reviewed, and compiled.

Figure 3-9. Email to Managers With Video Clip

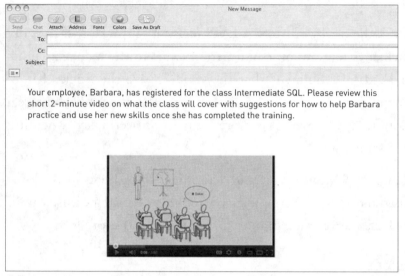

© Carnes and Associates, Inc.

TIE: Sticky Learning Community

Creating community and collaboration around your learning using social tools like Facebook or Yammer is a great way to support training transfer. Social tools can be used to supplement the content in an e-learning or live virtual class and provide a space for participants and course graduates to discuss what they've learned.

An advantage of using tools such as Facebook and Yammer is that they are very informal and user-friendly—trainees and graduates who may be reluctant to participate using other tools are more comfortable adding a short comment to a wall post, posting a photo, or just clicking "Like."

Instructors and designers can subscribe to an RSS feed for their learning communities, or simply log in regularly, to monitor discussions and other user activity, answering questions and correcting misleading or inaccurate information as needed. Perhaps the most important pitfall to watch out for with this kind of training platform is learners' tendencies to let discussions and other activities veer off topic or become counterproductive. Careful moderation of the community should prevent this.

Set up a Facebook or other learning community account that could be used for many different training programs. An email address is all that is required (be sure to use your work email address for this purpose, and not let the platform default to your personal email if it has already been entered in the system). Once the account has been set up, complete the profile information. The focus of the profile can be on the organization, the training department, or a specific class.

Set up a class-specific page, known on Facebook as a "fan page." The advantage of using a fan page is that people can be invited to the fan page without having to first establish a "friend" relationship with the page administrator. Upload a photo or logo to add visual appeal. Post class-related information. Separate fan pages might be set up for pre-training and post-training. The registration email can contain a direct link to the pre-training fan page, which could have information such as:

* technology specifications, or recommendations for compatibility with the e-learning or live virtual learning technology platform

* recommended or required pre-work reading or other activities

* icebreaker activity

* description of how this training supports the organization's mission, vision, goals, and strategy (see the Strategy Link TIE)

* tips for optimal learning, such as how to focus, review, and take quizzes

* "can-do" messages to motivate participants.

Options for a post-training fan page include:

* asking for success stories and lessons learned from practicing and using the new skills

* post-training team project

* discussion about how the newly acquired skills might advance one's career

* peer supporters sharing their perspectives on the training (see the A Little Help From Friends TIE).

Regardless of specific uses, it is a good idea to establish general rules for participating in the learning community. For example, community members should keep their communication respectful, relevant, short, and positive. The most effective learning communities facilitate the exchange of valuable information between participants. The focus is on the relationship between fellow participants, not between an instructor and trainees. Seed the community with questions and topics for discussion. Provide some conversation starters to get people talking, and check in regularly.

The most effective learning communities facilitate the exchange of valuable information between participants.

To use with e-learning

1. Establish a platform for a learning community dedicated to a specific class. Set up "fan pages" for pre-training and post-training or for other appropriate points in the training. Include a link to the pre-training fan page in the registration confirmation email participants will receive.

2. Introduce a project or discussion that will be hosted on the fan page at an appropriate point in the e-learning, and invite or direct participants to visit it. Provide a direct link to the page. Participation in the learning community will be more robust if the designer, a subject matter expert, facilitator, or other designated person moderates.

3. Participation in the learning community will of course increase if it is required rather than optional. However, tracking participation may have to be done manually if it cannot be done by the LMS.

Adaptations for live virtual training

1. Use a learning community fan page for pre-training introductions. In a pre-training email, ask participants to post a photo and introduction prior to the live virtual session. Include a screenshot(s) of the fan page at the beginning of the class.

2. Mention the learning community in the class. Explain any post-training or between-session assignments and provide the direct link onscreen and in the chat field. It is also a good idea to send a follow-up email with the assignment and the direct link. Otherwise, participants may realize too late that they did not copy the link when it appeared during the live virtual training.

Downsides

This TIE may not be effective if:

❖ Participants have a "check the box" attitude about their training. If this is the case, require that each participant contribute a certain number of posts.

❖ There are organizational restrictions for using a learning community. In this case, investigate opportunities to use an internal platform such as Yammer. Yammer offers a "Basic Network" option that is available for free.

Variation

❖ Use Facebook or another learning community as the platform for the class itself. Provide content, assignments, visuals, and facilitate discussions all within this virtual classroom. A class can be put together very quickly this way, as a temporary or permanent solution.

Figure 3-10. Social Media Tools and Their Uses

All social media is not alike. Different tools are best used for different purposes.

Social Media Tool	TIE	Use
Blog	Sticky Blog	conveying pre- and post-training motivational material, supplemental information, posts that contain significant amounts of content
Facebook and similar	Sticky Learning Community	hosting discussions and sharing information among learners, including links to useful websites, pre-training assignments such as icebreakers, and additional information and resources
Twitter and similar	Sticky Microblog	sharing short bits of information, reminders, and links to useful websites
Wiki	Sticky Wiki	learner collaboration to develop "how-to" information, such as a manual
Threaded Discussion	Threaded Discussion	hosting a discussion amongst many participants that shows the relationship of multiple replies on a topic related to the training content.

TIE: Sticky Microblog

Using a microblog such as Twitter can be a great way to connect with learners, remind them of what they learned, and provide tweet-sized messages of inspiration. Microblog messages, called "tweets," can help set the stage for learning transfer by signaling participants to think about how they will be able to use what they learn and when they might be able to practice it. A tweet beforehand could also remind participants to plan to close out applications and turn off their phones while taking the class. Tweets after training will remind participants to practice newly learned skills and knowledge, and could also recommend additional resources such as books and websites. After-training tweets could also remind participants to visit a social learning community or other after-training site.

Access to Twitter (*www.twitter.com*) is free to anyone, although as with any public site, it is not as secure as a company intranet. For a platform that is protected by a firewall, you can use Yammer (*www.yammer.com*).

Microblog messages can be one-way communication from trainers, or responses from participants can be expected or even required.

To use with e-learning

1. Decide on the best tool to use for sending out brief messages to learners. If the organization is already using an internal platform such as Yammer, this is the best choice. If not, you can use Twitter, but remember that Twitter is a public platform and should not be used if the information being shared is proprietary or confidential.

2. The training registration confirmation sent to the participant from the LMS should include a request for the participant to establish an account on Twitter or Yammer if they do not already have one.

3. Draft messages ahead of time, and use an external Twitter application (such as HootSuite—*www.hootsuite.com*) that will store messages and send them at predetermined times.

4. Ideas for messages include (keep in mind the 140-character limit):
    ❖ five ways participants can use this training
    ❖ useful website(s) to visit (Twitter will shorten the web address)
    ❖ brief explanation of how the training can advance participants' careers
    ❖ reminders of when and how to use a particular skill.

5. Once the messages have been drafted, decide how to deploy them. One option is to assign a *hashtag* to the messages and refer to it in the course. Hashtags are keywords that are preceded by the pound symbol (#). Tweets carrying the same hashtag are grouped chronologically into a discussion thread that is searchable within the system. For example, in a course on conflict management, ask trainees to search for the hashtag #ConMg for a particular message, such as one step in managing conflict that is most often overlooked.

6. It is a good idea for a coordinator or training administrator to monitor these discussions and be available to answer questions or spark dialogue.

Tweets carrying the same hashtag are grouped chronologically into a discussion thread that is searchable within the system. For example, in a course on conflict management, ask trainees to search for the hashtag #ConMg to keep up with tweets related to the course.

Adaptations for live virtual training

1. Between training sessions, use a microblog platform to send out homework reminders, recommended reading or websites, or short bits of learning content.

2. Consider using a microblog to form a sort of "backchannel" during training, in which participants can communicate with each other and ask questions of a moderator (preferably not the facilitator) to clarify or reinforce their understanding of the content.

Downsides

This TIE may not be effective if:

❖ Participants are unable to access microblog accounts during work time.

❖ Participants resist signing into a separate account to view their messages.

Variations

❖ Use rhetorical questions (where no answer is expected) rather than statements or discussions in the microblog posts.

❖ Involve trainees' managers by sending them the hashtag for the discussion thread.

TIE: Sticky Objectives

Instructional objectives usually state what the participant should know or be able to do at the end of the training. Getting participants to attain these objectives may be important for the trainer, and could be used in the research and design phases of course development. But for the participant and the participant's manager, "sticky objectives" that state what the participant should know or be able to do *on the job* are much more relevant.

A good training objective should state or imply three things: the skill, the condition, and the criteria. The *condition* refers to the condition(s) under which the participant should be able to perform the skill. The *criteria* refer to how often and how well the participant should be able to perform it. Criteria are usually one or more of the following: quality (100 percent accuracy) or quantity (number of projects or increase in productivity). The *skill* should be specific and measurable.

A "sticky objective" simply shifts the timeframe of the performance from *at the conclusion of training* to *on the job*. For example:

> *Good objective*: The participant should be able to use project management software on the job to develop schedules and timelines without assistance.

> *Bad objective*: The participant should understand how to use project management software.

In the first example, the skill is to develop schedules and timelines for real projects back on the job. The condition is using the specific project management software. The criterion is being able to do so without assistance. The second example identifies understanding project management software as the skill to be learned, but understanding cannot be measured, and there is no condition or criteria.

Here is another example of a good objective: The participant should be able to use WYZ project management software to track timelines and expenditures and to plan requirements, reducing work time for these operations by at least 25 percent.

The skill is using WYZ project management software; the condition is when managing projects. The criterion is reducing work time by at least 25 percent.

A "sticky objective" is an instructional objective that simply shifts the timeframe of the desired performance from at the conclusion of training to on the job.

To use for e-learning and live virtual training

1. Discuss proposed training with managers and subject matter experts, focusing on what the trainees need to know or be able to do *on the job*. How will they use and apply the skills and abilities in the course of their work? How will this improve their ability to do their job? What prompted this request for a training class? What are they hoping the training will solve or resolve? How can this be measured? What does success look like to them? The answers to these questions will guide the development of sticky objectives.

2. Design the training using instructional objectives in the usual way—defining the skill or knowledge the participant should know or be able to do at the conclusion of the training—as an *internal reference* to be used by the trainers. For some classes they may be one and the same, but in many cases the instructional objective may be different from the end performance goal.

3. Once the training is designed, review the instructional objectives and ask, "Are these the skills and knowledge that should be used on the job?" If not, revise them.

4. Use the sticky objectives in course descriptions and materials, and in communication to trainees and managers. Note: It may be that not all trainees

will use the skills in the same way. It may be necessary to provide several different versions of the objectives that are specific to certain job titles.

5. Use the sticky objectives for training evaluations. Level 1 (end of class) evaluation questionnaires should ask participants whether they intend to use what they have learned, referring to the specific skills as stated in the objectives. Level 3 (transfer) evaluation questionnaires should ask participants and their managers if they are using what they have learned, referring to the specific skills as stated in the objectives.

Downsides

This TIE may not be effective if:

❖ The skills and knowledge addressed in the training are not specific or measurable.

❖ The objectives are considered a formality by either the trainer or trainee, or both, and are not reviewed at the conclusion of the training or used in any type of evaluation of either the trainee or the training.

Figure 3-11. Sticky Objectives

Instructional Objectives

- Apply specific Techniques to Integrate Education (TIEs) to increase effective transfer.
- Practice incorporating TIE transfer strategies into e-learning and virtual classes.
- Share best practices and lessons learned to achieve high levels of training transfer.

Sticky Objectives

- Apply Techniques to Integrate Education (TIEs) to increase effective transfer of your e-learning and live virtual classes.

- Use the Transfer of Technology-Supported Training Model in classes you design.

- Incorporate best practices (and lessons learned) to achieve high levels of transfer.

TIE: Sticky Wiki

A wiki is an interactive webpage or site that allows users to post and edit content. The result is information that is maintained by these contributors. A popular example of a wiki is Wikipedia. A "sticky wiki" is a wiki that supports, reinforces, and otherwise extends the learning of a formal training course, making learning transfer quicker, easier, and more likely to occur. One of the biggest reasons that learning is not applied to the job is that the trainee does not have any assistance or support once the class is over. While the trainee's manager is usually the best source of this support, a wiki can also provide been-there, done-that support from knowledgeable contributors.

A wiki can be used to support an e-learning class or live virtual training several ways:

❖ as a place for FAQs to be posted and answered

❖ as a repository for class notes from both learners and instructors, or for class takeaways

❖ as a project site for collaborative class projects (see Action Learning TIE)

❖ as a place to discuss what has been learned in class

❖ as a "living manual" for how to do something.

The collaborative aspect of a wiki is the very essence of web 3.0 technology and presents excellent opportunities for interaction among participants, trainers, designers, subject matter experts, and anyone else interested in the content. The disadvantage of this open access is that anybody can post anything, whether or not they are knowledgeable and qualified. There are some ways to control access, however.

A wiki can be password-protected so that, for example, only those registered for a particular class or those who have received credit for a particular class have access. A wiki administrator can also specify editing permissions. For example, class participants in an entry-level class may only be able to view the wiki, while members or graduates of an advanced class would receive permission to edit its content.

Platforms for creating a wiki are readily available on the Internet, sometimes for free. Other applications such as Microsoft SharePoint include wiki functionality. Wikis can also be created and installed inside the company firewall. Consider how the wiki will be used and what types of information are likely to be posted.

One disadvantage of wikis is that they are not the best platform for discussions. To host conversations, consider using a microblog, blog, or learning community.

Learner participation in wikis will probably vary. Some learners may be hesitant to edit others' posts, so some encouragement may be necessary. It is a good idea to have an "owner" of the site who can monitor the content and encourage learners to contribute.

To use with e-learning

1. Determine the purpose of this sticky wiki and the nature of the content that is likely to be posted.

2. Source hosting options. If the wiki will be on a company's internal system, discuss options with IT. For public sources, search using terms such as "public wiki." Search "start wiki" for some excellent resources on starting a wiki.

3. Decide where in the e-learning course to introduce the sticky wiki. If the main purpose of the wiki is to answer FAQs, include a link on several different screens where questions are likely to come up. If the wiki will be used for success stories and disseminating tips and advice, the link and invitation to visit the wiki should appear toward the end of the course, as part of the content on "how to apply what you have learned."

4. If the wiki will be used for collaborative projects, the structure will need to be established.

❖ How will the collaborators be grouped? Can the LMS organize participants into groups as they register for the class?

❖ What accountability and monitoring of the wiki and the project will be needed? Who will do it?

❖ Will the project participation be graded?

5. Decide who the wiki administrator will be. While not time-consuming, it is best to have someone who can make regular visits to the site.

6. Start a "get acquainted" section of the wiki. Post a brief bio and photo. Ask others to do the same. It is amazing how this simple activity can break the ice for later sharing.

7. Remember that a wiki doesn't need to be text only. For ideas on using graphics in a wiki (and many other ideas), check out *www.wikiversity.org* and *www.wikispaces.com*.

8. Determine permissions. It's recommended that everyone be allowed to edit content. Find a volunteer such as a SME to help monitor and correct any misinformation, or make it the responsibility of the entire group. Note that the wiki can be set up to send the administrator a notification email when something is posted.

9. Invite course graduates to contribute to the wiki if the focus is on collecting valuable insights or maintaining FAQs. A course graduate may also be a potential "owner" of the wiki, to provide monitoring and oversight.

10. Include a "Like" button so participants and visitors can indicate which information has been useful to them.

11. As with most social media tools, it is a good idea to keep a close watch on how much the wiki is being used and publicize it as necessary to drive participants to it. Keep in mind that social media efforts to enhance learning transfer often fail due to lack of participation. Requiring participation—a certain number of contributions from each participant, or a graded assignment, for example—will ensure participation.

Adaptations for live virtual training

1. Decide how you want to use the wiki and at what point in the training it should be introduced. Just as with e-learning, a wiki can be a good place to post notes, slides, and other resources from live virtual training. If the chat log isn't too long, it could also be included. Invite additional comments and other contributions to create an accessible record of the live virtual class.

2. The wiki could be used to post between-session assignments. For example, one such assignment might be to apply one of the techniques presented in class, and to post a note on the wiki to share how it worked, recommendations for next time, and so forth. Remember that wikis are not the best discussion forums. To spark dialog around the training, use a threaded discussion.

A wiki can serve as a dynamic job aid that is updated by both trainees and facilitators.

Downsides

This TIE may not be effective if:

❖ Permission to contribute and modify content is limited to a few people, with everyone else having "view only" access.

❖ The learning content is not complex and doesn't lend itself to after-class sharing of lessons learned, advice, additional resources, and so forth.

Variations

❖ A wiki can be used *instead* of a class, especially if information-sharing rather than skill development is the primary goal of the class. It will be more accessible, available as needed, and much easier to administer than either an e-learning course or a live virtual training class.

❖ Use a wiki to present some of the information also included in the class—for example, content that participants may need to access on the job when performing the skill. Include a link to the wiki in the class. The wiki now becomes a dynamic job aid that can be updated with user experiences.

TIE: Strategy Link

Most trainers understand the importance of aligning training to business goals and results. Research studies have found that when specific linkages are identified between training content and business strategy, mission, and goals, rates of training transfer are higher.

Yet participants often begin an e-learning course or live virtual training without understanding why they are there, what they are going to learn, how what they will learn is important to their job, and how it is linked to their organization's business goals. Establishing these "strategy links" is important in enhancing learning transfer.

To use with e-learning and live virtual training

1. When designing the training, look beyond the specified skills and processes that are needed. How will this training help the organization or department accomplish their mission? Achieve their strategic business goals? Possibilities include

   ❖ increased customer satisfaction

   ❖ reduced expenses and therefore increased profitability

   ❖ increased sales and revenue

   ❖ increased employee engagement and reduced turnover (which in turn reduces expenses and boosts profitability)

   ❖ reduced exposure to lawsuits and consequences of legal noncompliance.

2. If possible, review the organization's strategic plan. Also review the external and internal websites for additional information and useful wording that will provide hints on how to link the training to business goals and overall vision. For example, if the first few lines of the website say, "We have believed for decades in building quality business relationships and making recommendations that have been proven over time," this is an

indicator of the business strategy. Two other examples: "We are committed to improving the quality, safety, and performance of our assets," and "We develop and build affordable communities so people have quality places to live."

Review the organization's strategic plan and marketing communication for useful wording that will provide hints on how to link the training to its business goals and overall vision.

---

3. Write down the links between organizational strategy and the skills or knowledge being taught. These may be evident or they may need to be thought through. Here are some examples:

   ❖ If the strategy is improving quality, safety, and performance, and the class is on conducting effective performance appraisals: Effective performance appraisals are linked with higher levels of employee satisfaction and better supervisor-employee communication. Higher levels of satisfaction and communication result in better quality work and lower levels of turnover, which increases the overall quality and safety of the work.

   ❖ If the strategy is developing and building communities so people can purchase affordable, quality homes, and the class is on effective communication skills: Project managers and line managers can save time and reduce costly errors by communicating effectively and efficiently. Reduced rework and increased productivity result in better quality housing at more affordable prices.

   ❖ If the strategy is building relationships and developing repeat business, and the class is on customer service: Customer service reps can use proven relationship-building techniques and strategies to build customer loyalty and increase repeat business.

4. Decide how to communicate the strategy link to participants. The easiest option is to include a strategy link statement with the learning objectives. Here are some tips:

5. Repeat the strategy link at various points during the learning. Good potential "strategy link points" are before and after skill practices, in discussions, and when introducing a new section of the learning material.

6. Make a short video (two to three minutes should be long enough) of the CEO or another senior leader outlining the business strategy and the link with this learning program. Include it in one of the early slides of an e-learning program. Show it with the objectives in a live virtual training class. If it is only possible for the CEO to do one video segment rather than program-specific videos, show the general video and demonstrate the specific strategy link for each course yourself with text or audio.

7. Record a message from the CEO or other senior leader, stating the strategy link. Include a link to this audio file in the pre-training registration confirmation. Use a photo with it to add visual interest. Send a copy to trainees' managers.

8. Ask trainees' managers to review the strategy link with their employees before or after the class.

Downsides

This TIE may not be effective if:

❖ The organization does not have a clearly-defined strategy or does not make it available for employees.

❖ There isn't a clear connection between the learning content and the strategy.

Variations

❖ In a live virtual setting, conduct a discussion to explore what participants believe the connection is between the training and the organization's mission, goals, and strategy. Be sure to have some of the resources described above (website copy or the organization's official mission statement) on hand to share.

❖ Have the CEO or another senior leader draft an email to participants specifically explaining how this training will support the mission, goals, and strategy of the organization.

TIE: Thank-You Note

This TIE is so simple, it hardly needs explaining. People love to be thanked—for their hard work, for their contributions, for their assistance, or just for showing up. A simple thank you helps a person feel important, and sends the message that what they have done is valued. From a training perspective, a thank you implies that the trainer understands the difficulties the participants may have had in finding time for the learning event, and in overcoming the challenging nature of the learning material.

Besides the benefits already mentioned, a thank you provides a valuable opportunity to reinforce key learning points and to remind learners about what they need to do back on the job to apply the training.

Make sure to thank trainees specifically for something—such as making time to participate in the learning event, making the effort to depart from the old way of doing things, or allowing themselves to open up to a new way of thinking.

To use for e-learning and live virtual training

1. What do you specifically want to thank trainees for? For taking time out of their busy day to participate in the learning event? For hanging in there when the learning was challenging? For trying out a new skill or departing from their same old way of doing things? The thank you should also include a brief summary of key learning points, how the skills learned will help the organization and department achieve their business goals, and what the trainee should be doing on the job to reinforce or practice what they have learned.

2. Determine how the thank-you email will be sent. While a thank-you message sent automatically by the LMS is okay, the email will have more impact if it comes directly from someone such as a respected senior leader.

3. While email is the obvious choice for a quick and easy medium, there are other options. Voicemail may have more impact than email, and can lend a more personal touch. A higher-impact option is to send a handwritten note. A handwritten note is time consuming and may not be practical, but if the class was small this could be a feasible option for lending more sincerity to the message.

4. You will want to send the thank-you message no later than one week after the training is concluded.

Downsides

This TIE may not be effective if:

❖ The thank you is very general in nature, and does not include reinforcement of key learning points and a reminder of what to do now that the learner is back on the job.

❖ The thank you is sent long after the conclusion of the learning event.

❖ The learners regularly receive high volumes of email. (Choose a medium through which the message will not be "lost in the crowd.")

Variations

❖ Send a thank-you note prior to the learning event, and include the learning objectives and an explanation of how the learning will help trainees do their jobs better. In this case thank them for registering for the class or for having the courage to learn a new way of doing something.

❖ Ask trainees' managers to send the thank you. Ask them to explain in their note ways that the training material will help trainees in their jobs.

❖ Send a thank you in the midst of a multiple-session live virtual class. In this case thank the participant for "hanging in there" and working hard, and remind them of any practice homework they need to do.

❖ Send the thank-you note with the certificate of completion.

TIE: Threaded Discussion

Trainee interaction plays a big part in whether or not e-learning sticks. Not only does interaction with other trainees and an instructor or subject matter expert increase their understanding of the subject itself, it also increases their understanding of how they will be able to use the training back on the job.

Many university online classes make heavy use of threaded discussions. Very few corporate e-learning classes do. Yet this is a relatively simple, low-cost way to allow trainees to interact with each other and with the content expert, resulting in higher levels of learning transfer.

Threaded discussions provide several advantages over verbal discussions that take place in the physical or virtual classroom. The written medium allows time for thinking before responding so that the overall quality of the discussion is usually better. The written medium also does not have the "air time" constraints that are always present with verbal discussions. Good points are often lost in verbal discussions because of lack of opportunity to speak. The written discussion also makes it easier for non-native English (or any other language) speakers to participate. It can also, of course, be archived for later reference.

Threaded discussions are preferable to other online tools often used for discussion. Most blogs provide opportunities for readers to comment on writers' posts, but these comments can only be displayed in chronological order. If a conversation is sparked by readers' comments, it can be difficult to see the relationships of such comments to each other because of their linear arrangement.

A threaded discussion begins when a question is posed which starts the thread. Participants reply to the original question and to each other, and a discussion begins. Types of questions which work best as threaded discussion starters are

❖ open-ended, that cannot be answered with a "yes" or "no." Yes or no questions can work as long as they are expanded by follow-up questions. For example: "Have you ever been involved in a hazardous material incident? If so, what was the extent of the damage and how was it handled by the emergency management personnel?"

❖ Socratic. Named after the Greek philosopher Socrates, these types of questions have long been respected means of expanding learners' assumptions, reasoning, and perspectives.

❖ about prior experiences related to the topic.

Figure 3-12. Socratic Questioning

There are six types of Socratic questions:

- Conceptual clarification
  - Why do you say that?
  - What exactly does it mean?
  - Can you give me an example?
  - Are you saying...or...?
- Probing assumptions
  - This seems to assume...
  - If this is so, then please explain...
  - What would happen if...?
- Probing rationale, reasoning, and evidence
  - How do you know this?
  - Can you give me an example?
  - What do you think this causes...?
  - Why is...happening?

- Questioning viewpoints and perspectives
  - What are some other ways of looking at this?
  - What is the difference between...and...?
  - What would...say about it?
  - Why is...better than...?
- Probing implications and consequences
  - Then what would happen?
  - How could...be used to...?
  - What does...fit with what we have learned about...?
  - Why is...important?
- Questions about the question
  - Why do you think this question is important?
  - Does this make sense?
  - What else should be asked?

Source: ChangingMinds.org, "Socratic Questions."

To use for e-learning

1. Identify key concepts in the content that may need further clarification or can be expanded with discussion.

2. Identify or review the learning objectives to determine specific questions about application.

3. Locate the best software platform to host the threaded discussion. Many LMS platforms have threaded discussion features, although they may not have been activated. Consult the IT department or LMS administrator. Otherwise find other options by searching for "threaded discussions" or "threaded discussion platform." The threaded discussion should be accessible through a link posted on one or more slides.

4. Determine who will moderate and lead the discussions. This person can be a training instructor, course designer, subject matter expert, or line manager. Since most of the discussion will be conducted by participants, the leader simply needs to respond to questions and make sure the discussion stays focused on the topic. Extensive knowledge of the topic is not necessary. The maximum amount of time required to lead a discussion group of five to seven discussion threads should be 30 to 45 minutes, total.

5. Require participation in threaded discussions as part of the class and state this in the opening slides of the course. The most straightforward way to do this is to require a certain number of posts during a specified time period. For example, to complete the class, each participant must post at least three times in seven days. Unless the LMS software does this automatically, the facilitator will need to track participation to ensure that posting requirements are met before class credit is given.

6. Post suggestions and guidance for discussion posts. For example:

   ❖ Show you are reading others' comments by referring to them in your own posts.

   ❖ Agree or disagree with others' posts and explain why.

   ❖ Share outside resources, such as books and articles, related to the topic.

   ❖ Do not use the discussion area as an online gripe session. Keep comments constructive.

7. Incorporate the discussion into the learning module(s). Introduce the discussion on a slide at the appropriate point in the course and provide a link to it. Encourage participants to contribute to the discussion or

simply read what others have written before proceeding with the rest of the course. If possible, in the discussion area include a link that takes the participant back to the slide in the class that they left.

Adaptations for live virtual training

1. In the live virtual classroom, pose a question onscreen and ask participants to respond in the chat. The chat feature doesn't allow for the threading of replies, however. If the technology platform allows for breakout groups, these can also be used for discussions, although they aren't the best platform for a threaded discussion because it isn't possible to show replies to replies. For best results, post a link to the threaded discussion platform and ask participants to use that to engage in discussions during class, instead of using chat or breakout groups in the virtual classroom.

2. Host before-class or after-class discussions. Consider specifying that a certain number of posts within a certain time period must be completed in order to receive credit for the class. If a discussion is to be held between training sessions or afterward, a threaded discussion feature in an LMS is the best option and may be able to track participation too.

Downsides

This TIE may not be effective if:

❖ Discussion topics are sensitive and participants are reluctant to share their views. It may be helpful to clarify who will and will not be able to view the discussions.

❖ Participants stray from the topic and the facilitator does not keep them on track.

❖ There is no incentive for participation. Usually requiring a certain number of posts provides the necessary push if this is the case.

TIE: Transfer Certificate

Some participants are "certificate collectors." They keep certificates of training completion and perhaps even display them in their cubicles or offices. Other participants could not care less about the certificate itself, but when they take a training class they expect to receive credit for it in some tangible way.

Just as training objectives should indicate the desired on-the-job skill use, the certificate or class credit should be an acknowledgement that the skill *has been applied on the job* and not that the class has merely been completed. Awarding certificates for applying learning gives the trainees an incentive to demonstrate their ability to use their newly gained skills and knowledge on the job.

Ideally the trainer or manager should observe trainees on the job and verify that skills learned in training are being used. However, this takes time that most trainers and managers do not have. A more realistic approach is to require the trainee or their manager, or both, to respond to a short survey about how they are applying what they have learned. At the very least, this kind of "application survey" can serve as a reminder to use the skills if they are not already being used, and present an opportunity for managers and trainees to discuss specific ways to apply the learning. The survey can also provide trainees and their managers with resources that enhance learning transfer, such as links to learning communities, wikis, and blogs.

Awarding certificates for applying learning gives the trainees an incentive to demonstrate their ability to use their newly gained skills and knowledge on the job.

To use for e-learning and live virtual training

1. Make sure the learning objectives reflect on-the-job application rather than end-of-class learning. Revise them as necessary. Refer to the Sticky Objectives TIE for more information.

2. Determine how application can be demonstrated and who will be involved. If a survey will be used, decide whether it will be administered to trainees, their managers, or both. Will completion of the survey be sufficient for class credit, or is a certain score (number of answers that indicate transfer) necessary to pass? If only participants will be surveyed, will they be forthright in their responses?

3. Check the capabilities of the LMS. How much support can it provide in terms of sending and grading surveys? Can they be sent automatically several weeks after a trainee completes the class? Is it possible for survey responses to be scored to determine pass/fail? Can class credit be awarded and a certificate sent automatically when surveys are completed? If the LMS isn't capable of doing this, you could develop the survey using a web-based survey tool and send a post-training email with a link to the survey.

4. At the beginning of the class, explain when and how credit will be given.

5. At the end of the class, after the final quiz or exam if there is one, outline the process again for receiving credit for the class. If a survey will be used, indicate when trainees should expect to receive it, if their managers will also be asked to complete it, and the criteria for passing.

6. Develop the survey. The questions in the survey should be closely linked to the learning objectives, and should prompt trainees to identify specific ways in which they have applied the skills. While open-response, essay-type questions are time-consuming to review, they may provide the best way to get the needed information. Consider using open-ended questions for the first few classes and review the responses. Use these responses to develop multiple-choice questions to use for later classes.

7. It may be useful to develop a series of follow-up emails that remind participants (and their managers, if they are involved in this process) to take the survey or provide other demonstration of application.

8. It is ideal for the LMS to automatically award credit for the class based on the answers given in the survey. If it doesn't have this functionality,

however, the time required to do this manually is quite minimal when balanced with the benefits to be gained.

Downsides

This TIE will not be effective if:

❖ Trainees need credit for class completion, for certification or other external requirements (although this could be done in addition to the transfer certificate).

❖ The LMS is not capable of automating this process, and class sizes are too large to perform it manually.

Variations

❖ Email participants and informally ask how they are using what they have learned.

❖ Collect participant feedback immediately or soon after training and award a "commitment to transfer" certificate.

❖ Award a transfer certificate not linked to receiving credit for the class.

Figure 3-13. Requirements for Transfer Certificate

You've finished the class – BUT

Please read this important information.

To receive credit, your supervisor must complete the short survey (s)he will receive in approximately 3 weeks, verifying that you have practiced and are using what you have learned.

TIE: Virtual Tutor

A virtual tutor (also known as a pedagogical agent, coach, or avatar) is a cartoon, video, or photographic image of a person who guides the trainee through the learning content providing guidance, instruction, and commentary. The virtual tutor personalizes the learning experience, increases engagement, and reduces trainee boredom. Research has found that trainees work harder, apply themselves more to the learning, have higher test scores, and improve their transfer rates by as much as 30 percent when there is a digital assistant present. This virtual tutor should communicate verbally if the technology allows; comment bubbles are also acceptable. The tone of the conversation should be friendly and informal. Comments that are overly formal ("The learner is counseled to remember ….") reduce learning and transfer, as do comments that are overly informal ("Hey dude, let's get going"….). A friendly yet professional conversational tone ("Let's begin with a simple idea"…..) leads to the best learning and transfer. This is especially true with learners who are inexperienced with the topic. Two or three virtual tutors provide variety and reduce audio monotony.

Figure 3-14. Virtual Tutor

Research has found that trainees work harder, apply themselves more to the learning, have higher test scores, and improve their transfer rates by as much as 30 percent when there is a digital assistant present.

To use with e-learning

1. Determine how the virtual tutor(s) will be used in the e-learning program or virtual classroom. Will it be providing additional instruction, serving as a guide, or coaching the learner by anticipating reactions and providing responses ("You may not have answered this question correctly because... Please keep in mind that...")?

2. Decide how this virtual tutor(s) should look. While photos and videos of an actual person are more realistic, they may also distract the learner if the person reminds them of someone they know. A cartoon is less likely to cause this reaction.

3. Seek out options for a virtual tutor. Some authoring applications include avatar images to choose from. Some websites have avatars and characters available for free or for purchase. A browser search using terms such as "avatars," "animated avatars," "free avatars," and "free cartoon characters" will yield the most current offerings. Be sure to keep copyright restrictions in mind. Be aware that avatars and cartoon characters are popular in gaming and informal social networking communities so it may take some time to find appropriate choices. Marketing or advertising departments within the organization may already have images that can be used as a virtual tutor.

4. Solicit feedback from colleagues, members of the target population, and others as to whether the virtual tutors seem appropriate for the learning material and whether the audience will be able to relate.

5. Write the "script" for the virtual tutor and incorporate it into the e-learning storyboard and design. If PowerPoint is used for the storyboard, the comments section can be used for the virtual tutor script. Be sure to introduce the virtual tutors by name ("Hello, I'm Barbara and I will be

your guide.") Text-to-speech software is quite realistic and can be used for the voice(s). Alternately, record the voice(s) using voice types that are a good match for the visual appearance of the tutor(s).

Adaptations for live virtual training

1. In the live virtual classroom the instructor serves as the virtual tutor so there is no need to create a digital personality to fill this role. However, a distinctive image included on the slides will probably enhance the overall experience for the learner.

2. If the digital personality will talk, be sure the virtual class platform will accommodate the sound files and if so, in what form or file type. Determining this ahead of time will save time later.

Downsides

This TIE may not be effective if:

❖ The culture or atmosphere of the organization is so formal that digital characters would be seen as childish and unnecessary.

❖ The goal of the training is to get through it as quickly as possible, resulting in the desire for a very pared-down, simplistic course design.

❖ The training design does not clearly distinguish the virtual tutor's role, so that trainees are confused about its purpose and the message it is sending.

Variations

❖ Introduce the virtual tutor to the learner in the registration confirmation email or other pre-class communications. The virtual tutor can be used to give the participants a preview of the material, build interest and motivation, demonstrate how the training links with company strategy, and comment on the usefulness of the training.

❖ Use the virtual tutor in post-class email communication, to provide reminders of key learning points and links to additional resources, and to encourage practice and application of skills.

❖ Incorporate the virtual tutor in other TIEs such as the Sticky Learning Community, Pop-Up Reflections, Feel-Felt-Found, Do Now, and Thank You.

TIE: What's Wrong With This Picture?

We know that showing trainees the correct way to perform a skill is an important part of a good instructional design. Showing trainees the *wrong* way to perform a skill can also be an effective teaching method. In several different studies, identical trainings on a variety of topics were presented to two groups of trainees. The only difference in the paired trainings was that in addition to demonstrations of the correct way to perform the skills, one of the groups was shown demonstrations of the incorrect way to perform the skills. The group that was shown examples of incorrect behavior achieved significantly higher rates of transfer than the group that was shown only the correct examples. This technique is called an "error-based example." It is important to show enough contrast between the correct and incorrect examples so that it is apparent which is which. The error-based example could even be presented in a humorous way to help make the distinction.

To use for e-learning

1. When researching module content and skill demonstrations, seek out subject matter experts to answer questions about incorrect usage of the skills you will be teaching.

   ❖ What are typical errors people make when performing this skill?

   ❖ What are one or two things that someone should avoid doing when they perform this skill?

   ❖ What has happened or could happen when someone doesn't do this the right way?

2. When designing the e-learning module, identify skill demonstrations as usual: video clips, graphics, or text-based descriptions of how to perform a skill or a sub-skill.

3. Next design the error-based example. For best results, use the same media that was used to demonstrate the correct example.

4. Decide how to present the error-based example in relation to the correct example. Here's an example: In a self-paced e-learning module on how to conduct a performance appraisal discussion, a video of how *not* to do it was broken into several three to four minute segments. Each segment was followed by two slides. The first slide asked the learner questions about what they observed and used a radio-button response tool. The second slide explained what was done wrong (that is, explained the correct answers to the questions asked on the previous slide). After this series of slides, a complete video of the correct way to conduct a performance review was presented, followed by questions with radio-button responses and then by an explanation of what was done well.

When developing error-based examples, seek out subject matter experts to answer questions about incorrect usage of the skills you will be teaching.

Adaptations for live virtual training

1. Live virtual platforms have some limitations for skill demonstrations, but there are usually workarounds so that short videos and live webcam demonstrations can be used in addition to, or instead of, photos and graphics. For example, in a live virtual version of how to conduct a performance appraisal discussion (see example above), the video segments were followed by a live discussion of what was done wrong and what was done well.

Downsides

This TIE may not be effective if:

❖ There is not enough contrast between the correct example and the error-based example.

❖ There is not a clearly defined, correct way to perform the skill.

❖ The error-based example is not followed by an explanation of what was done incorrectly.

Variations

❖ Viewing the correct and incorrect video segments and responding to the questions after each segment can be used as between-session homework in the live virtual environment. If the platform allows it, repeat one or more of the video segments in the live virtual session for added reinforcement.

❖ Include the consequences of incorrect skill use in addition to the incorrect skill performance. Some examples:

> ❖ In safety training, show a machine malfunctioning.
>
> ❖ In sales training, show an angry customer hanging up on the sales rep.
>
> ❖ In performance appraisal training, show an employee's reaction after having a counterproductive conversation with his manager.

TIE: Wrap It Up

Because self-paced e-learning, and to some extent live virtual training, have higher levels of learner control than face-to-face training, the ability to reflect on one's learning strategies, to know how to overcome blocks to learning, and to understand one's preferred approaches to learning, can significantly increase training transfer.

Knowing *how* to learn (also referred to as *metacognitive skills* or *cognitive ability*), can involve independent goal-setting, effective time management, good test-taking habits, and techniques for absorbing and processing learning content. Students who receive as little as half an hour of training on metacognitive processes have been found to outperform students who do not receive this training.

Consider developing a stand-alone module on self-directed learning skills. This module can then be made part of an onboarding program, or it could be pre-work for other e-learning classes. Such a module would include how to set learning goals, how to review e-learning slides and content, understanding one's learning style and how to use it most effectively in a self-directed e-learning environment, and how to take quizzes and tests.

With or without this metacognitive, learning-how-to-learn training, learners who use tools referred to as "content wrappers" and "quiz wrappers" achieve higher levels of learning and application. These wrappers can easily be added to existing or new e-learning content and live virtual training.

With repeated use of these content wrappers and quiz wrappers, trainees' skills at preparing for and taking quizzes will improve, as well as their ability to analyze errors they have made.

Content wrappers and quiz wrappers can increase learning retention and transfer by improving trainees' critical thinking and test-taking abilities.

To use for e-learning

1. At the beginning of the e-learning class, provide some tips on active reading, similar to active listening, and suggest that they think about key points and take notes as they read. Provide instructions for using the note-taking tool that is available in most e-learning platforms.

2. At the end of a section, include a slide that asks the learner to write down the three most important steps or concepts to remember in that section. In the next slide, reveal the three steps or concepts that they should have identified. You may want to adjust the information presented in each section so that there are not more than three key points made.

3. Be sure to include a quiz at the end of each section and an overall exam for the entire class. If possible, provide the correct answer immediately after each question.

4. After each quiz, provide "quiz reflection" questions which prompt the trainee to think about the mistakes they made and to plan their learning strategies for the next module. You can ask them to enter their responses and proposed learning strategies in the LMS if you like.

5. Before the next quiz, instruct the participant to review their responses to their last post-quiz reflection and to keep these in mind as they take this quiz.

Adaptations for live virtual training

1. At the end of a section or at another convenient stopping place, ask participants what they believe are the three most important things to remember about what has been covered. Ask them to respond verbally, in the chat space, or make a note to themselves if a worksheet has been provided. Do not use a poll here—it is important that participants think about this on their own rather than respond in a multiple-choice format. Then reveal the right answer. Plan to do this two to three times during a 90-minute class, depending on the content.

2.   Use quizzes to test learning, at the end of the class or at the end of key learning points. If the technology platform does not have a quiz feature, use the polling feature. Provide the correct answer after each question. It is not necessary to capture test scores for this to be effective. After each quiz, provide quiz reflection questions which prompt the trainee to think about the mistakes they made and to plan their learning strategies for the next module. Suggest that they take notes (provide a worksheet), and tell them they will be asked to refer back to these before the next quiz.

3.   Before the next quiz, ask participants to review their responses to their last post-quiz reflection and to keep these in mind as they take this quiz.

4.   Alternately, send participants links to quizzes after a live virtual session. Be sure to provide post-quiz reflection questions and prompts to review their quiz strategies before taking another quiz.

Downsides

This TIE may not be effective if:

❖ The learning content is so simple that asking them to identify key concepts is redundant.

❖ Participants will not take notes on key content points or quiz responses.

❖ Participants have a "get through it" attitude about the training and are not interested in thoroughly absorbing the material.

❖ The material is so complex, or is presented in a less-than-straightforward way, so that trainees are not able to identify key points or correctly answer many of the quiz questions.

Variations

❖ Use content and quiz wrappers with some but not all learning modules. For example, use them initially with all modules and gradually reduce use as learners' learning skills improve.

❖ Use content and quiz wrappers only with complex content; that is, content that requires more critical thinking, problem solving, and decision making.

❖ Use one without the other. For example, using quiz wrappers in certification courses may be especially useful, while using content wrappers in courses that present very complex information could help learners break down the concepts into more understandable chunks.

❖ Ask participants to make a mind map, flowchart, or drawing of the key points of a particular topic or issue.

References

ASTD. (2011). *2011 State of the Industry Report*. Alexandria, VA: ASTD Press.

Bean, C. "Avoiding the Trap of Clicky-Clicky Bling-Bling." *eLearn* Magazine. Accessed June 2011 at http://elearnmag.acm.org/archive.cfm?aid=1999745.

Bettelheim, B. (1987). *A Good Enough Parent*. New York: Knopf.

Bontis, N., Hardy, C., and J. Mattox. Diagnosing Key Drivers of Job Impact and Business Results Attributable to Training at the Defense Acquisition University. *Defense Acquisition Research Journal* 18(4):348–367.

Bozarth, J. (2010). *Social Media for Trainers*. San Francisco: Pfeiffer.

Broad, M., and J. Newstrom. (1992). *Transfer of Training*. Reading, MA: Addison-Wesley.

Burke, L., and H. Hutchins. (2007). Training Transfer: An Integrative Literature Review. *Human Resource Development Review* 6(3): 263–296.

Carnes, B. (2010). *Making Learning Stick*. Alexandria, VA: ASTD Press.

ChangingMinds.org. "Socratic Questions." Accessed February 26, 2012 at http://changingminds.org/techniques/questioning/socratic_questions.htm.

Colvin Clark, R. (2011). *E-Learning and the Science of Instruction*, 3rd ed. San Francisco: Pfeiffer.

Costa, G., J. Morais, N. Silva, and A. Sotero. (2010). Knowledge Versus Content in E-Learning: A Philosophical Discussion. *Information Systems Frontiers* 12(4): 399–418.

Cowan, C., E. Goldman, and M. Hook. (2010). Flexible and Inexpensive: Improving Learning Transfer and Program Evaluation Through Participant Action Plans. *Performance Improvement* 49(5): 18–27.

E-Learning! Magazine. (2011). "Less Instructor-Led, More Computer-Based." Accessed at http://www.2elearning.com/trendlines/article/less-instructor-led-more-computer-based.html.

Flavell, J. H. (1979). Metacognition and Cognitive Monitoring: A New Area of Cognitive-Developmental Inquiry. *American Psychologist* 34: 906–911.

Granger, B., and E. Levine. (2010). The Perplexing Role of Learner Control in E-learning: Will Learning and Transfer Benefit or Suffer? *International Journal of Training and Development* 14(3): 180–197.

Groner, D. (2002). How to Overcome Self-Inflicted Obstacles to Learning. *National Underwriter Life & Health* 106(38): 33.

Hopkins, T. (2010). "The Feel, Felt, Found Strategy." Tom Hopkins International: The Official Blog of Sales Champions. Accessed at http://www.tomhopkins.com/blog/presentation/the-feel-felt-found-strategy.

Hutchins, H., and L. Burke. (2007). Identifying Trainers' Knowledge of Training Research Findings—Closing the Gap Between Research and Practice. *International Journal of Training and Development* 11(4): 236–264.

Johnson, D., and B. Carnes. (1988). *Making Training Stick*. Minneapolis, IN: Creative Training Techniques.

Johnson, R., H. Gueutal, and C. Falbe. (2009). Technology, Trainees, Metacognitive Activity and E-learning Effectiveness. *Journal of Managerial Psychology* 24(6): 545–566.

Kirkpatrick, D. (1998). *Evaluating Training Programs*. San Francisco: Berrett-Koehler.

Kirkpatrick, J., and W. Kirkpatrick. (2010). ROE's Rising Star: Why Return on Expectations Is Getting So Much Attention. *Training and Development* 34: 34–38.

Latham, G., A. Stajkovic, and E. A. Locke. (2010). The Relevance and Viability of Subconscious Goals in the Workplace. *Journal of Management* 36(1): 234–255.

Mansi, G. (2011). "An Assessment of Instant Messaging Interruptions on Knowledge Workers' Task Performance in E-Learning-Based Training." PhD diss., Nova Southeastern University. Accessed at http://udini.proquest.com/view/an-assessment-of-instant-messaging-pqid:2376421111/.

Mattox, J. (2006). "The Current State of Scrap Learning and Manager Engagement." KnowledgeAdvisors.com. Accessed January 14, 2012 at http://www.knowledgeadvisors.com/archives/the-current-state-of-scrap-learning-and-manager-engagement/.

Marquardt, M. (2011). *Optimizing the Power of Action Learning: Real-Time Strategies for Developing Leaders, Building Teams, and Transforming Organizations*. Boston, MA: Nicholas Brealey Publishing.

Osborn, C. (2010). "Learning Management Systems in Small and Mid-Sized Organizations: Usage and Features." Presented at the BizLibrary ALIGN Conference, St. Louis, MO, 2010.

Sloman, M. (2005). The Changing Role of the Trainer. *Industrial and Commercial Training* 37(7).

Strang, K. (2011). How Can Discussion Forum Questions Be Effective in Online MBA Courses? *Campus-Wide Information Systems* 28(2): 80–92.

Varnadoe, S., and N. Rabinowitz. (2011). Learning Now: Five Digital Strategies to Bring Learning Into 2011. *Training and Development* 65(4).

Weissbein, D.A., J.L. Huang, J.K. Ford, and A.M. Schmidt. (2011). Influencing Learning States to Enhance Trainee Motivation and Improve Training Transfer. *Journal of Business and Psychology* 26(4): 423–435.

Wick, C., R. Pollock, and A. Jefferson. (2010). *The Six Disciplines of Breakthrough Learning.* San Francisco: Pfeiffer.

Van Zile-Tamsen, C. M. (1996). "Metacognitive Self-Regulation and the Daily Academic Activities of College Students." PhD diss., State University of New York at Buffalo.

About the Author

Barbara Carnes is a pioneer in the field of training transfer. She co-authored the first book on the subject, *Making Training Stick*. More recently she has authored *Making Learning Stick* and *Making Training Stick: A Training Transfer Field Guide*, as well as numerous articles and webinars on training transfer and related topics. Barbara is a consultant, trainer, speaker, and writer. Before founding Carnes and Associates over 25 years ago, Barbara was a member of the training staff for Sprint. She is listed in the national registry of Who's Who, and has presented at national and international training conferences including the American Society for Training & Development, TechKnowledge, DevCon, the Canadian Society for Training & Development, Learning 3.0, and Creative Training Techniques.

Barbara has a PhD in human and organizational systems from Fielding Graduate University, where her dissertation was on training transfer. In addition to training trainers, writing her mini-newsletter *Sticky Notes*, and offering a Making E-Learning Stick Certification, Barbara teaches graduate courses for Webster University and the University of Phoenix. Her websites are *www.maketrainingstick.com* and *www.makeelearningstick.com*.

Index

W

Y